First published in the United Kingdom in 2013 by
Portico Books
10 Southcombe Street
London
W14 0RA

An imprint of Anova Books Company Ltd

ISBN 978-1-907554-82-7

A CIP catalogue record for this book is available from the British Library.

10 9 8 7 6 5 4 3 2 1

Printed and bound by CPI Group (UK) Ltd, Croydon, CR0 4YY.

Research and additional text: Colin Salter
Illustrations: Damien Weighill

Picture credits: All photos are courtesy of Batsford, with the exception
of page 28, which is courtesy of Rex Features.

This book can be ordered direct from the publisher at
www.anovabooks.com

the
# joy
*of*
# pubs

Frank Hopkinson

PORTICO

# CONTENTS

Pub Records
74

Pubs in Films
82

Pub Crawls
116

Pubs with Ghosts
128

Pubs in Literature
96

Pub History
148

Pubs in the News
140

# Introduction

I always feel uneasy going to my brother's house. It's not because he makes me feel unwelcome, or that he's stingy with the hospitality – there's an amazing variety of drinks and snacks you can buy from the pound store these days. No, it's because he lives in what was once the Britannia Arms in Usk, Monmouthshire. Sitting in his front room you can feel the weight of small history weighing on your shoulders – the celebrations that have been held, the news that's been passed, the landmark events in everyone's lives shared in the pub – first dates, last dates, terrible news, joyous celebrations, stag nights, fights, chance meetings, fond farewells. It's like living in an old church or an old village school – you are interfering in people's ability to come back and remember. A pub is part of the fabric of a community and it feels like you must have closed off the ability to come back and soak it all up again.

That feeling of timeless continuity is the essential difference between a pub and a bar. A pub has a comfortable, worn-in feeling, like a favourite armchair that's been in the family for years and been re-upholstered many times. A bar is an impermanent, fly-by-night operation subject to the whims of fashion that caters for a narrow range of clientele and haircuts. Bars don't generate affection the way pubs do. You wouldn't get two old men with a Jack Russell playing cribbage in a bar. Dogs are hopeless at cribbage.

This book is a tribute, an affectionate look at many aspects of that quintessential British institution, the pub. The fact that they are disappearing at an alarming rate is a news story and statistic that is so often quoted that it begins to lose its impact. Some say it's 18 a week, some say 12, whatever the figure, it's too many. They are as much a part of our national history as any National Trust-owned country house. There is a rich history in the naming of pubs that goes back to medieval times. In fact, there is more history in British pubs than the whole founding of the USA. Rewind 900 years and you could have walked into Ye Olde Trip to Jerusalem in Nottingham and ordered an ale – waited 300 years – and Christopher Columbus would still not have set sail for America. And the glory of British pubs is that you can still walk into Ye Olde Trip to Jerusalem, order an ale and drink a toast to the prospect of civilization 2,000 miles to the west. (If pubs had been invented in America, we'd have had the Pub Hall of Fame by now, and Mel Gibson would have produced a film about how the English tried to prevent pubs from coming into existence.)

Not all pubs have history, though. Take the flat-roofed pub. It's a general rule of thumb that flat-roofed pubs are the most dangerous. You won't get any horse brasses or inglenook fireplaces in the flat-roofed pub. This is because they're most likely to be found close to a 1960s housing estate. If you decide to go in, you won't get served before Big George – even if it's your turn to catch the barman's eye and Big George has just hoisted his tracksuit bottoms over his hairy backside and wandered up to the heavily dented bar.

This is one of the unwritten rules about getting served in a pub – there is a hierarchy of who is likely to get served next and it's pretty universal. At the top of the tree is the Regular. The order is: 1. Regular, 2. Attractive girl with cleavage, 3. Attractive girl, 4. Threatening-looking guy, 5. Tall bloke, 6. Average height bloke, 7. Average bloke with beard, 8. Short guy, 9. Short scruffy guy with beard, 10. Tourist.

As we're British we like to be served in turn, but we don't like to make too much of a fuss when we're not. Unless it gets ridiculous. I once avoided a fight in a pub in Hereford because I was desperate to impress a girl from Hereford Art College. The succession of short blokes that came up to the bar – all with droopy John Newcombe / Mexican bandit moustaches, it was the 1970s – got served in front of me. I wanted to appear cool, and so to have caused an argument would have blown it. So I smiled and waited as the line of stocky, unsmiling little fellas ordered their pints. It was only in the early 1980s, after the Iranian Embassy siege in London, that I discovered the SAS were based in Hereford. And after I read Andy McNab's book, *Bravo Two Zero*, I learned that the favoured form of moustache for the SAS was the John Newcombe and that you didn't have to be built like Captain Hurricane to qualify. I'd been in one of their favourite pubs giving way to a succession of diminutive killing machines.

This is one of the things we all treasure – a pub anecdote. Having grown up in Worcestershire in the 1970s, going to the pub was the thing you did on a Friday and Saturday night – there was little alternative. It was either the cinema – one screen, usually Disney – or the pub. There were so many – and we had a car. It was an ocean of opportunity. We could go to the Red Lion in Great Malvern, the Chase in Colwall, the Swan in Upton, the Farmers Arms in Castlemorton, the Three Kings in Hanley Castle, the Pheasant in Welland, the Wellington in Colwall (where Trevor swears he once saw the Electric Light Orchestra's Jeff Lynne), the Unicorn, the Morgan, the Nag's Head, the Lamb, the Bluebell, the Beauchamp, the Swan with Two Nicks in Worcester, or the Herefordshire Arms (good pool table, often not busy, and not quite in Herefordshire).

You remember the times you had too many pints of Robinson's Old Tom and attempted a worrying game of darts, where actually hitting the board made you roar with laugher. (Old Tom, brewed in Stockport, is surely the real reason that the BBC relocated to Salford Quays.) You remember the pub crawls, the landlords who refused to serve you and the ones where they'd turn a blind eye if you looked 17. You met up with friends, talked rubbish and never met any girls. With the fanaticism of youth, we developed such a love for Wadworths 6X we actually drove to the brewery to look at it one time. Yes, just look at it and to prove the theory that it might taste better the closer you got. So now, when my teenage children aren't interested in going down the pub and stay at home killing zombies or watching endless repeats of *Game of Thrones*, I'm horrified. They're wasting their heritage.

Although pubs are still closing, some are fighting back, thanks to the combined pressure and assistance from CAMRA, the Prince's Trust and Community Interest legislation. The villagers of Battisford in Suffolk were dismayed when their local pub, The Punch Bowl – an inn since 1727 – closed in 2009. The Parish Plan, undertaken at the time, clearly demonstrated how much it was valued within the local community. A group of local residents began the task of acquiring the lease in order to re-open it as a Community Interest Company. It was the same story with the Sorrel Horse in the village of Shottisham, also in Suffolk, where the owner wanted to develop land around the pub for housing. Villagers mobilized support and raised a massive £450,000 to buy and renovate their pub.

Pubs Researcher (he's getting a card printed) Colin Salter has dug up many stories for this book, but one of them shows that there might be a more diverse future for our pubs. All over Britain, thousands of women are meeting up in their local on a weekly or monthly basis – to sew and knit. Tilly Walnes, a contestant on the 2013 BBC series *The Great British*

*Sewing Bee*, goes to a sewing bee at her local pub. Knitting bees too are thriving in the informal and now smoke-free environment of the boozer. Pubs have long been the home of award-winning gastronomy, and pub quizzes have helped bring punters back in through the doors.

In African villages, the neutral ground where everyone can come and meet and discuss issues, is in the shade of the meeting tree. In Britain we have the pub. You don't get developers in Africa saying "you know, if we cut this meeting tree down we could squeeze in a nice development of huts here", it is sacred ground. We should maybe start thinking the same way about pubs.

**Frank Hopkinson, 2013**

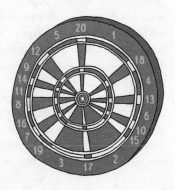

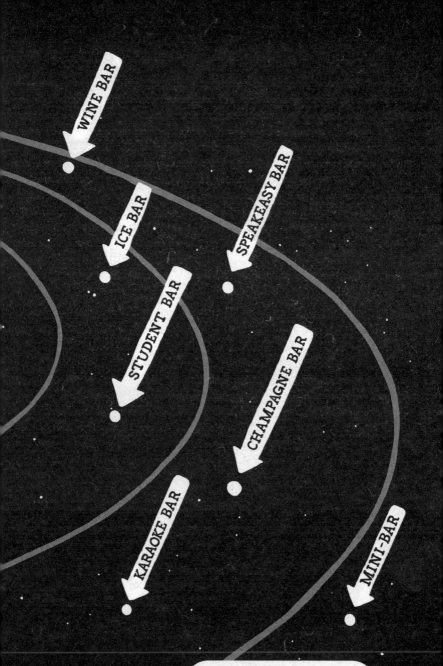

**THE PUB GALAXY**

# Pub Games

Is nothing sacred? It turns out most British pub games are imported. Card games arrived from Egypt, via Italy and France; skittles were played in Holland and the low countries, long before they arrived in the 17th century; bar billiards came from Belgium via Russia, and table football from Italy in the 1930s. Finally, it was pool which arrived from America in the 1960s. Getting the jukebox to work properly with a series of deft thumps and bangs is not considered an official pub game – it's a pastime.

### 🍾 Cards

Card games are played beyond the confines of public houses, but it was in the inns, bars and hostelries of 14th-century Europe that the game spread like wildfire. Card games are believed to have been invented by the Mamelukes in Egypt around the 12th and 13th century with a complete pack of 52 ancient cards from that period turning up in the Topkapi Palace Museum in Istanbul in 1939. The cards were divided into four suits: swords, polo sticks, cups and coins. From Egypt the game spread to Italy courtesy of Venetian traders. By 1377 the City of Florence was trying to ban a variety of card games associated with gambling. The four suits were interpreted differently in each country. Traditional German packs had hearts, acorns, bells and leaves; the French had hearts, pikes, clover and a roof tile; Switzerland had shields, acorns, roses and bells, while Spanish cards had cups, swords, coins and clubs. Cards used in Britain evolved from the French design.

PUB
FACT

Pubs haven't always had the liberal opening hours they have today. Before 1988 they opened from 11am to 2.30 or 3pm and then from 6pm to 10.30 or 11pm. The gap in the middle of the day wasn't a Victorian rule for a striving nation. Closing pubs after lunchtime was part of the Defence of the Realm Act (DORA) brought in during World War I. It was designed to get workers back to their places of work sober for an afternoon shift.

## Cribbage

In the 1968 Gaming Act, cribbage was the only card game that was allowed to be played 'for small stakes only' on a national level. It is said to have been invented by Sir John Suckling (1609–42), a character straight out of the 'Blackadder' mould. He was a poet, gambler 'the greatest gallant of his time', a wit, womaniser and serial cheat. He produced cards with his own secret marks and got them sent to gaming houses around the country. He adapted a game known as 'Noddy' and called it 'Cribbage' with cards tossed into a metaphorical crib. He popularised the game at court and hence it became an acceptable game for the proletariat to play. His downfall was being implicated in a plot to free Thomas Wentworth, The Earl of Strafford, from the Tower of London. He fled to Paris and poisoned himself in 1642 – presumably when he couldn't think of a cunning plan.

 ## Everyone Plays Darts

Along with the dwindling number of pubs are the dwindling number of pub dartboards. If ever there was a game that is most associated with a British pub, then it's darts. The traditional London Board, with doubles and trebles and '20' at the top is what everyone is used to. However, this hasn't always been the case. Pub games historian Arthur R. Taylor has tracked down many regional varieties over the years, including a Grimsby Board which has numbers 1–28, a Burton Board (traditional numbering but no trebles), a Tonbridge Board (no outer bull and the trebles occupy the doubles position), a Yorkshire Board (similar to the Tonbridge), a Wide Fives board (for those with maths challenges, scoring is 5, 10, 15 or 20), a Narrow Fives board (the same but with smaller doubles and trebles) and the Manchester Board (only 10 inches across). One of his greatest regrets is that he never found a Norfolk Board.

### On the Norfolk Boards

Like many old dartboards, the Norfolk dartboard was made of elm and about 10 inches across. Part of the reason that dartboards evolved as circles and not squares is that they were cut as sections of a tree trunk. The scoring area of the Norfolk Board was about five or six inches in the centre of the board made up of concentric circles, very much like an archery target. The bull scored four, the next ring scored three, and then the last ring or 'magpie' was worth one. None survive.

### Nightmare on Elm Board

One of the problems with the traditional elm dartboard is that they dry out. The modern boards can be left hanging for 365 days of the year but if you have a wooden board it needs to be soaked. So landlords would have to stick it in a water butt or an old butler's sink after a day's play. Quite often they were still dripping wet when they were brought out to play again the next day. This treatment would rust the wires and so boards hardly lasted more than a year. The consequences of allowing a board to dry out were terminal: the wood would warp, twisting the wires out, and the wood would be too hard for the darts to stick in. One of the reasons that old-fashioned darts were like weighty offensive weapons is that they had to stick into a block of elm.

### Mancs Love Little Audrey

The London Board may be the (almost) universally accepted dartboard, but there are still pockets of resistance clinging on in the north. The Manchester Board is just 10 inches across with tiny doubles at the edges, a bull, an outer, but no trebles. The bull is also known as 'Little Audrey'. On the Manchester Board the number 4 occupies the coveted 20 position at the top of the board and only the 19 segment is in the same position as the London Board. With characteristic Mancunian swagger, the London Board is known as the 'Big Girl's Board' while the hometown board is referred to as 'Little Audrey'. Some pubs in Manchester are said to have both boards, but the most famous Manchester pub of all, the Rovers Return, only has a Big Girl's Board – along with big Audrey Roberts.

## A Literary History of Pub Darts

It would make the perfect 'specialist subject' round for *Mastermind* –
the literary history of pub darts isn't going to threaten world paper stocks.
Jane Austen might have mentioned sheds (as noted in the companion title:
*The Joy of Sheds*) in her work, and in *Pride and Prejudice* Elizabeth Bennet is
staying with the Gardiners in a Derbyshire inn when she hears the shocking
news of Lydia's elopement, but there's no mention of darts, the range of
pub snacks or information on 'the guest ale'. Look up that great working
class writer D. H. Lawrence and his only connection with darts is during
a bullfight in 'The Plumed Serpent'. It's left to E. Temple Thurston and his
book *The Flower of Gloucester*, a *Three Men in a Boat*-like tale of leisurely
cruises on Cotswold canals that we get an account of pub darts.

Thurston recounts that he and his boatman played a game of darts at the
Red Lion in Cropredy, Oxfordshire against a couple of farm labourers for
'four glasses of ale'. "The board was painted black and all about the face of
it were little holes where darts had entered. It was a game they played to
while away a lazy hour."

PUB
FACT

Dominoes were introduced to Britain by French
prisoners of the Napoleonic wars, who had
nothing else to do with their day than carve their
own sets out of old bones. The original game
dates back to the Song Dynasty in China, around
the 12th century AD.

### 🍺 Pub Darts Games

There's the traditional 501 game ending on a double, but there are other games that can be played on a dartboard that don't involve a nostalgic trip back to a primary school maths tests.

Blocker: One player is the blocker, the other is the scorer. The blocker goes first and tries to eliminate all the high number scores by landing a dart in them. The scorer follows on and can only score points in the non-blocked numbers. So the blocker would try and hit 20–19–18, and then the scorer following would try and get the maximum number by aiming three darts at 17. The game continues until the blocker has blocked all 20 numbers. Then the score of the scorer is added up and the roles reversed.

Blind Killer: Best played with four or more players; a neutral scorer gives each player their own number(s) on the board anonymously. Then he chalks up the numbers and players take it in turns to eliminate the numbers by landing in them. Each number has 10 lives until eliminated. Because it's blind, players don't know who they're trying to eliminate. There can even be a bit of bluff-ology by landing near your own number. As a variant, players can be asked to hit a certain number five times before they get their licence to kill.

PUB
FACT

Dartboards can be made out of all kinds of
materials; wood, wound paper, helically-wound
sisal AKA the 'bristle' dartboard and plasticine.
The first chairman of the National Darts Association,
Ted Leggatt, made dartboards from plasticine.

Cricket: Two teams or two players. The batsmen have 10 wickets (as you'd expect). They throw first and try and score 40 or above. Everything above 40 counts as runs, so a score of 54 counts as 14 runs. If they don't reach 40 they lose a wicket. The bowling side have the next three darts and try and score bulls, which count for two wickets, or outers, which count for one. So if the first batsman scores 39 on the board and the bowler that follows him gets an outer, the batting side is 0 for two wickets. All kinds of extras can be added on and the games rules can be changed to make it harder or easier (i.e. scoring above 20 or 30 or 35).

## Skittles

Skittles arrived in Britain via Germany and the low countries. The history of the game is helped by official attempts to try and ban the lower orders from playing it when they should be out on the land doing their serf duties. Edward III banned the playing of 'Kayles' which was like skittles but played with a cudgel instead of a ball to knock the pins over. Around a hundred years later, in 1477, Edward IV banned all kinds of games that had evolved from it, including cricket, skittles and rolly (played with a half-sphere to make it more difficult), in favour of archery practice. Skittles has since splintered off with all kinds of regional variations: Old English, London Skittles, Long Alley, Devil Among the Tailors, Hood, Northants Skittles, Leicester Skittles, Half Bowl and Daddlums.

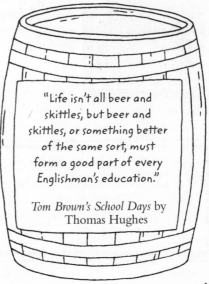

"Life isn't all beer and skittles, but beer and skittles, or something better of the same sort, must form a good part of every Englishman's education."

*Tom Brown's School Days* by Thomas Hughes

## West Country Rules

The archetypal skittles game, West Country Skittles, is played with nine heavy wooden pins. Players have three attempts to knock over all nine with a wooden ball. If they knock them all over on the first go, they are re-set and so players in theory can score 27 points per round.

With the variation known as Long Alley, players have to throw a log or 'cheese' and hit the pins with just a single bounce.

London Skittles also have a wooden cheese to throw, but this is discus- (or cheese-) shaped and weighs between 4 and 6 lb. Instead of counting the number of skittles knocked down, players add up the number of cheeses it takes to knock over the nine.

Half Bowl or rolly is a lot more complex than the brute force of skittles and involves bowls-like skill. Players have to throw a hemi-spherical bowl which has to curve round an end pin before it can curve back and knock the pins down.

## Bar Billiards

Bar Billiards arrived in the UK via an international route. David Gill, an English businessman, was enjoying a walking holiday on the Franco-Belgian border in the early 1930s when he decided to stop in at an auberge for a cheeky little Stella Artois. In the corner of the bar he spotted a few of les reguleurs enjoying a billiards-like game. They were potting balls into a rabbit warren of holes to score points. The high-scoring holes had a precariously placed mushroom on one side. If they knocked it over, catastrophe. Nul points. After 20-or-so minutes there was a clinking sound as a bar came down and stopped the balls from being used again and that was it, game over – or jeu fini.

The Belgians had gone crazy for Billiards Russe (Russian Billiards). Gill took the idea back to England and with anti-Russian sentiment running high, cleverly inserted the word Bar instead of Russian and a new British pub entertainment was born.

### Jersey Boys

The Bar Billiards World Championship is held every year in Jersey (The Crucible of Bar Billiards). Since 1981, Jersey has produced 11 World Champions and there has been no winner from outside the British Isles in that time.

### Bar Billiards Rules

Players take it in turns till they fail to pot a ball. If a white mushroom is knocked over, the player's break score is lost; if the black mushroom is knocked over, a player's entire score is lost. To finish the game, the last ball has to be potted directly into the 100- or 200-point hole after banking off one side cushion. The black mushroom guards the 200-point hole.

### The Pub Quiz: Question 1 – Where did it all Begin?

Despite its recent appearance – compared to Bat & Trap that's been around since the 15th century – the history of the pub quiz is a very under-researched subject. They are thought to have begun in the mid-1970s but

unlike the clamour to claim the title of Oldest Pub, nobody seems too fussed to claim the title of Oldest Pub Quiz. A 2009 survey by the British Beer and Pub Association estimated the number of pub quizzes run every week in Britain is around 22,500. Only 29% of Scottish pubs charge an entry fee for their quiz night, 71% are free.

> Despite being limited to just 19 minutes, expert bar billiards players can run up staggering scores. In 1984 Keith Sheard notched up 28,530 at the Crown and Thistle in Headington, Oxford.

## Another Great Export

Reflecting the Victorian era, when Britain invented and codified games and exported them round the world, the pub quiz has been exported to Ireland, America, Holland, Belgium, France, Australia and New Zealand. Big business has taken over the American pub quiz trade, with one national quizmaster – Geeks Who Drink – supplying a 'conflict resolution and arbitration phoneline' to resolve disputes in quizzes. It sounds like The Big Bang Theory down the pub.

## Saturday Night's Not Alright

Pub quizzes are used to boost traditionally quiet nights of the week. A 2009 survey by the DP Quiz website of 230 Scottish pubs found that 40% of them offered quiz nights (close to the 42% national average). Thursday was the most popular night (31%), Monday and Sunday next (18%), Tuesday (15%), Wednesday (12%), Friday (6%) and none were held on Saturday. Starting times varied, with a late start preferred north of the border. Most started between 9 and 10pm (52%), many started between 8 and 9pm (35%), a few started before 8pm (10%) and hardly any started after 10pm (3%).

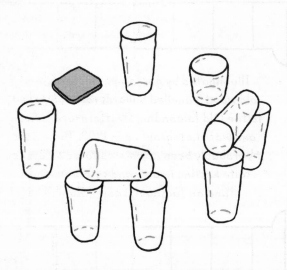

Illuminated by gas lamps, this burnished
old wood-panelled billiards room belonged
to the Old Falcon Inn, Stratford-upon-Avon,
and was photographed in 1900. These days
it's probably been converted to a conference
suite hosting health and safety seminars
and on Tuesdays, Ladies' Zumba.

# Pubs on TV

It's a well-known statistic that you're more likely to have an accident in the car driving you to the airport than the plane flying you out of it. But when it comes to pubs in TV soaps, the high odds of being involved in a hostage siege, robbery, punch-up, arson attack or tragic accident should make you think twice about walking through the doors. Thank goodness for the pub in *Early Doors*, where nothing dramatic happens...ever.

## Eastenders – The Queen Victoria

Truly the monarch of TV pubs, The Queen Victoria reigns supreme at 46 Albert Square and in millions of homes. Seen four evenings a week in Britain and on English-speaking channels throughout the world, it must be the envy of every real-life bar, attracting millions of regulars every night. Successive battles for the tenancy and ownership of the bar have been central to plot lines since *Eastenders* was launched in 1985. Like all good East End pubs, it has witnessed a procession of crimes and celebrations. Death is one of the Vic's regulars: Tom Clements died of a heart attack in the pub toilet in 1988, and since then three of its landlords have been murdered, one of them on Christmas Day. Christmas has never been a good time to go to the Vic – Den Watts served Angie divorce papers on that day in 1986. The Queen Vic isn't the only soap pub to suffer serious fire damage in a dramatic storyline, but it has been the victim of arson twice – once in an insurance scam by Grant Mitchell in 1992, and once by Grant's brother Phil in a revenge attack in 2010.

## Not on Your Nellie – The Brown Cow

In 1974, London Weekend Television launched *Not on Your Nellie*, a new sitcom starring much-loved music hall entertainer Hylda Baker. Baker played Nellie Pickersgill, a teetotal Lancashire woman helping out in The Brown Cow, her father's pub in Chelsea. Cue hilarious culture clashes between traditional northern values and fashionable southern ways. Wendy Richard (later a regular in *Eastenders'* Queen Vic) played a busty barmaid, and The Brown Cow's customers included Gilbert and George, an early example of a sitcom gay couple. The show ended abruptly and acrimoniously midway through its third series when Baker, aged 70, sued LWT – she had broken her leg in rehearsals after slipping on a pool of spilled beer.

## River City – The Tall Ship

BBC Scotland's answer to *Eastenders*, *River City* is set in the criminal underworld of the country's Clydeside ship-building community, so naturally the pub at its heart is called The Tall Ship. The first series, in 2002, began with a celebration there, the wedding of the pub's owners Eileen and Tommy Donachie. But like so many soap opera watering holes, The Tall Ship eventually became a victim of arson. It was destroyed in a massive and deliberate explosion in 2012, when murderer Raymond Henderson turned on the gas and left the zippo lighter of his victim flaming on the pub floor, watched by audiences from Glasgow to Sydney.

## Minder – The Winchester Club

*Minder*'s dodgy used-car salesman, Arthur Daley, predated three-wheeler-dealer Del Trotter of *Only Fools and Horses* by a year. Arthur fancied himself as a more gentlemanly sort of crook, however, and drank at a members-only establishment, The Winchester Club, owned by long-suffering barman Dave Harris. Dave tried to run an honest house and was a good listener to Arthur's troubles with his wife, 'Er Indoors. But he often had to overlook the questionable legality of Daley's schemes as he passed messages between Daley and his minder Terry. Five different doorways around London played the part of the entrance to the Winchester – six if you count the short-lived 2009 revival – while the interior remained constant, a film set in a studio in Hammersmith.

In 1964, Alfred Hitchcock visited Granada Studios (home of *Coronation Street*) to see old friend Sidney Bernstein who'd worked with him on *Rope* (1948). He obviously couldn't resist the pull of Newton & Ridleys on draught. Laurence Olivier was desperate to appear in the pub. Barmaid Bet Lynch — actress Julie Goodyear — revealed on *Desert Island Discs* that: "He told me he wanted to play a tramp with a plot line that he came into the Rovers Return for me to throw him out."

## Coronation Street – The Rovers Return

Just as Corrie has seen off threats from *Crossroads* and *Eastenders*, so The Rovers Return has seen other Weatherfield pubs come and go – The Farriers Arms, The Flying Horse, The Laughing Donkey, The Queens and The Weatherfield Arms have all played supporting roles to the Grande Dame of soap pubs. In 2010 a huge explosion, the fresh start of choice for so many soap pubs, put paid to the latest rival, The Joinery, causing a tram to crash down onto the street in the process. On that occasion the Rovers Return acted as an emergency room for the victims, but the pub has itself twice suffered the standard soap opera disaster – ratings-boosting fire damage. In 1986 faulty electrics were to blame; and in 2013, in a second attempt to write barmaid Sunita Alahan out of the show, arson gutted the place. The pub has also been struck by a heavy goods vehicle (in 1979), and a significant number of natural births and deaths have happened on the licensed premises. On no occasion has Betty's legendary hotpot, the best-selling item on the Rovers' pub-food menu, been to blame. The pub has already had six different licensees this century, as many as it had between 1960 and 2000. Many believe the first, Annie Walker, is still the best.

## Emmerdale – The Woolpack

The Woolpack Inn in Emmerdale can claim to be the second oldest TV pub after *Corrie*'s Rovers Return. Since 1998 *Emmerdale* has been filmed on a purpose-built village set, but when the series was launched in 1973 the exterior of the Woolpack was filmed at the **Falcon Inn** in Arncliffe, Littondale. When Yorkshire TV decided to move location filming to the **Commercial Inn** at Esholt, they had to introduce a plotline involving the discovery of subsidence in the original building. Subsidence has been the least of the Woolpack's worries. Like all good soap pubs it has experienced a range of disastrous fires: an accident with some sparklers in 1998 burnt the place down, only five years after a fireball engulfed the building when an airliner crashed into the village. Then in a fierce storm on New Year's Day 2004, a rotten chimney breast crashed through the roof of the bar, killing Tricia Dingle. Unusually for a country pub, it has also been the scene of a classic soap opera hostage situation, when in 1978 the generously moustached original landlords Amos Brearly and Henry Wilks, were held at gunpoint by thieves.

**Only Fools and Horses – The Nag's Head**

One of the advantages of a pub in a drama is that the flow of alcohol encourages characters to drop their guard. No surprise therefore that in *Only Fools and Horses* Del Trotter was a regular customer in his local pub, The Nag's Head. Where better to pass off his dodgy goods to unsuspecting customers? Unfortunately one of his most frequent victims was the gullible barman Mike Fisher. In one episode Del sells him a hairdryer which is in fact a paintstripping gun. Del is told that he's "run up enough slates to roof the building". Unfortunately for pub fans, Del's finest barside comedy moment – the one when he disappears from view past a raised barflap – took place not at The Nag's Head but in an upmarket bistro. Real life pubs filmed as The Nag's Head exterior included **The Middlesex Arms**, South Ruislip and **The Waggon and Horses** in Bristol.

### Shameless – The Jockey

The grittily dysfunctional comedy drama *Shameless* has a suitably seedy pub to match, The Jockey, a run-down 1960s bar on the fictional 1960s housing estate of Chatsworth in Manchester. You're as likely to be sold Ecstasy from behind the bar as alcohol. For most of its TV life, The Jockey has been run by various members of the Maguire criminal dynasty – notably Jamie and his wife Karen, a barmaid for the previous licensee Jez. In such a lawless place it's no wonder that the pub has been torched twice: once by pyromaniac Marty Fisher, and once with a Molotov cocktail thrown by Victor, a sacked chef. Before a purpose-built set was constructed, scenes were filmed in **The Wellington** (known locally simply as the Welly) in West Gorton, Manchester.

## Hollyoaks – The Dog in the Pond

The Dog in the Pond has been at the centre of the storylines ever since *Hollyoaks* was launched in 1995. Back then the owner was 1970s glamrock singer Alvin Stardust, in the character of Greg Andersen, and since his early departure the owners and tenants have mostly been members of the Osborne and Costello families (Sadly not members of Mudd, the Sweet, Showaddywaddy or the Rubettes). The pub was briefly renamed The Jolly Roger until Nev Ashworth, the proprietor at the time, realised that it had made the bar a focus for the village's gay community. It's a dangerous place, in which there have been several shootings. In 2011 landlady Heidi Costello was killed and a year after that so was her son Riley. Of two other landlords, Darren Osborne was only wounded, in 2007, and his father Jack only faked his death to avoid gambling debts. In keeping with soap tradition, a disastrous fire at The Dog in 2006 was an excuse to kill off five regular characters.

## Men Behaving Badly – The Crown

If ever a sitcom needed a pub it was *Men Behaving Badly*. **The Crown** literally fuelled the antics of Gary and Tony over six series of the quintessential 1990s laddish comedy. The final trilogy of special episodes of the show in 1998 was named Last Orders, and drinking lager until closing time was central to the lives of both badly-behaved men. The Crown had two landlords during the lifetime of *Men Behaving Badly*. Les dribbled, was rude to customers and offered departing customers a goodbye gherkin. His hapless replacement Ken only got the job through a family connection with the brewery's personnel manager, and had never managed a pub before – an innocent abroad of whom it would not take Gary and Tony long to take advantage. Shortly after Ken's appointment Tony, like a kid in a sweetshop, wangled employment at The Crown as a barman.

##  Ballykissangel – Fitzgerald's Bar

In a series set in a quiet Irish village, the pub was always going to be the centre of the drama. The very first episode of *Ballykissangel* saw new priest Father Peter Clifford clash with Assumpta, the beautiful but irreligious landlady of Fitzgerald's Bar. The Irish form of the village name, Baile Coisc Aingeal, means 'the village of the fallen angel'. The story of their inevitable love affair ran for three seasons before Assumpta was electrocuted by the pub's faulty wiring and died in Peter's arms. The pub itself survives as the self-styled Most Famous Bar in Ireland – the 200-year old former Fountain Hotel in Avoca, Co Wicklow, now of course known as 'Ballykissangel Country'.

## Life on Mars / Ashes to Ashes – The Railway Arms

Over the course of two series, *Life on Mars* delighted in playing mind games with its audience – was Sam Tyler mad, dead, or in a coma; or had he really travelled back in time to 1973? All along we had the sense that Gene Hunt's local pub The Railway Arms in the fictional Stopford area of Manchester was something more than it seemed to be. Its barman, Nelson, spoke with two accents – his own Mancunian one and the Jamaican patois his customers expected – and he dispensed wisdom with double meanings, applicable both to Sam's immediate 1973 problems and to his metaphysical predicament. Sure enough, we discovered at the end of the third series of the sequel Ashes to Ashes that The Railway Arms was a supernatural portal between purgatory and paradise, to which Hunt guided the souls of dead policemen who were ready to accept their death and cross over. Nelson was a sort of St Peter. Therefore the pub should really have been called The Cross Keys (see page 59).

## The League of Gentlemen – The Mason's Arms

The mercifully fictitious northern town of Royston Vasey (actually the real name of veteran comedian Roy 'Chubby' Brown) is the creation of the dark comedy quartet *The League of Gentlemen*. It has a local shop for local people, and of course a local pub, the real-life **Mason's Arms** in Hadfield – a milltown appropriately situated on the edge of the Dark Peak in the Peak District National Park. On TV the pub is best known as the venue for a performance by faded 1970s glamrock band Crème Brûlée, whose former rhythm guitarist Les McQueen is a Royston Vasey resident wistful for old glories.

## Heartbeat – The Aidensfield Arms

*Emmerdale* met *Dixon of Dock Green* in the 1960s rural police drama *Heartbeat*, which ran for a remarkable 18 years. Goathland in North Yorkshire was used as the fictional village of Aidensfield, and The Aidensfield Arms, the village pub at its centre, was portrayed by the **Goathland Hotel**. The log fire in the lounge bar of the Aidensfield Arms was said to have been kept alight ever since Queen Victoria sheltered there during a storm in 1860. This was a version of a genuine local story told of the nearby **Saltersgate Inn**, where 200 years ago the publican lit the fire to prevent discovery of the body of a murdered customs officer buried beneath the grate.

## Pobol y Cwm – Y Deri Arms

*Pobol y Cwm* ('people of the valley') is the BBC's longest-running soap opera in the Welsh language. Broadcast on BBC Wales since 1974, it transferred to the new Welsh-language channel S4C in 1982, while production remained in the hands of the BBC. From the first episode the Cwmderi village pub, Y Deri Arms, has been the focal point for a soap characterised by realistic, unsensational storylines. It couldn't last. In 2008 it had its dramatic fire, but caused by faulty electrics rather than the usual arson or revenge attack. The pub reopened in different premises soon afterwards and remains at the heart of the program, which is filmed in the real valley of Gwendraeth in South Wales.

### The Royle Family – The Feathers

We are introduced to The Feathers in the opening episode of *The Royle Family* when we hear that Dave is doing a disco there for his ex, Beverley; Dave is portrayed by Craig Cash, who later co-wrote pub sitcom *Early Doors*. Too often the Royles are trapped on their sofa watching TV, and any suggestion that they might go out to the pub is generally overcome by lethargy. As a result we have never seen The Feathers. But perhaps in Jim Royle's mind it's enough simply to know that his local exists, a promise of potential happiness should he ever decide to get off his a\*\*\* and go.

### Early Doors – The Grapes

Although the local pub is an essential location in any sitcom, surprisingly few are actually centred on one. *Early Doors* was a very honourable exception, revolving entirely around the blocked toilets and lovelorn staff and drinkers of the fictional Manchester pub The Grapes. *Early Doors*, co-written by Craig Cash, was populated with real people – chaotic, shambolic, defiantly unglamorous – and they were given a bar to match. Landlord Ken and his clients lived ordinary lives with ordinary problems, which they faced with wry, grim humour. No plane crashes or arson attacks ever troubled The Grapes, only the persistent problem of fag ends in the urinals and the fear that one day the brewery would turn The Grapes into a 'fun pub'.

### Doc Martin – The Crab and Lobster

Port Isaac in Cornwall, which plays the part of the village of Port Wenn in *Doc Martin*, is no first timer in the world of TV locations. The remote and picturesque fishing village has also appeared in *Poldark* and *The Shell Seekers*. The village's pub **The Golden Lion** became Port Wenn's hostelry The Crab and Lobster. The Lion would have been quite at home in *Poldark* – it has a secret passage which once allowed smugglers to escape the forces of law and order.

##  Bottom – The Lamb and Flag

Drink was central to the characters of base comedy *Bottom*. Rik Mayall's Ritchie got drunk at the mere suggestion of alcohol, while Ade Edmonson's Eddie had, he claimed, only been drunk once – it was just that he'd never sobered up. Their local, The Lamb and Flag (barman Dick Head), was the backdrop to the start of many crude and doomed attempts to persuade women to sleep with them. One running gag introduced in the first episode saw them attacked whenever they tried to enter The Lamb, not by women but by dogs aroused by the pheromone spray they had hoped would pull the opposite sex.

## Last of the Summer Wine – The White Horse

Holmfirth, the Yorkshire mill village around which *Last of the Summer Wine* was filmed, is a strange case of life imitating art. Many of the locations used for the program have taken on their fictional names (for example Sid's Café) or made up new ones to secure their connection with Summer Wine Country (such as the Wrinkled Stocking Tearoom). But **The White Horse**, whose interiors and exterior were regularly used in the program, is a genuine piece of Holmfirth history. These days The Horse trades heavily on its Summer Wine down-to-earthiness – 'more shirehorse than Shergar' – but, built in 1830, it was one of a few buildings to survive the catastrophic flood when a dam burst above the village in 1852. (Something that will probably happen in *Emmerdale* before long).

> "I said to the wife, 'Guess what I heard in the pub? They reckon the milkman has made love to every woman in this road except one.' And she said, 'I'll bet it's that stuck-up Phyllis at number 23'."
>
> *Max Kaufman*

## The Bill – The Bear's Head, Canley Arms, Elcott Arms, Seven Bells, The White Swan, The Scales

*The Bill* remains Britain's longest running police procedural drama with 27 years to its credit before being axed in 2010. In the course either of investigation or celebration, the officers of Sun Hill Police Station had occasion to visit an impressive number of pubs over the years – The Bear's Head, Canley Arms, Elcott Arms, Seven Bells, The White Swan and The Scales to name but a few. Like all good soap operas *The Bill* employed the plot device of a major fire as a means of writing out six characters in 2002 – although the fire destroyed not a pub but the station itself. Five years later officers requisitioned a pub as a control centre when Sun Hill nick was taken over by armed hostage-takers, in the course of which DC Perkins managed to set fire to the police canteen.

## Inspector Morse – Most Pubs in Oxford

A list of Oxford pubs patronised by Inspector Morse would fill a separate book. Beer was both his strength and his weakness; and alcohol abuse led to his fatal heart attack. The opening episode 'The Dead of Jericho' featured two city centre pubs: **The White Horse** in Broad Street, and – in its fictional guise as The Printer's Devil – **The Bookbinder's Arms** in Jericho, the publishing district of the city. The nearby **Jericho Tavern** was where Morse drowned his sorrows in Episode 2 'The Secret World of Nicolas Quinn'. The White Horse appeared again in two more episodes, 'The Wolvercote Tongue' and 'The Secret of Bay 5B'. The latter also included a visit to **The King's Arms** on Holywell Street – in real life the last pub in Oxford to open its doors to women (in 1973).

Finally, outside **The Victoria Arms**, a country pub in the village of Marston, Morse quoted A.E. Houseman's poetry while enjoying a last sunset and a drink with Lewis in the final episode of the series, 'The Remorseful Day'.

## Gavin and Stacey – The Colcott Arms

Although the action in *Gavin and Stacey* flitted between Barry in South
Wales and Billericay in Essex, all the filming was done in and around the
Vale of Glamorgan. **The Colcott Arms** in Barry had to swallow its pride
and become an English pub in which Smithy conducts the weekly quiz.
As question master he gets so drunk that he reads the questions to himself
and blurts the answers out loud, much to the horror of Gavin's father,
quiz regular Mick.

## Rebus – The Oxford Bar

Detective Inspector Rebus, a grumpier, more jaded, Scottish version of
Inspector Morse, shares Morse's reliance on good beer, and his drinking
den of choice is **The Oxford Bar** on Thistle Street in Edinburgh. Thistle
Street exists, a quiet backwater mostly occupied by boutique shops selling
designer fashion and decorative goods. The Oxford is a real pub amongst
these establishments, untouched by fashion or decoration (unless you
count a slice of the original flagpole from Murrayfield Rugby Ground
proudly framed in the bar).

## Past Orders

Fans of Channel 4's *Time Team* are familiar with the archaeologists' regular
retreat to the pub for a pint or two at the end of a hard day's dig. Channel 5
took the idea a step further in 2012 by bringing the whole dig to the pub.
For *Pub Dig* they dispatched TV's best known beer belly Rory McGrath to
four historic pubs where, at the end of a hard day's drinking, he and *Time
Team* veteran Paul Blinkhorn would retreat to an archaeological trench for
a dig or two. The pubs in question were: **The Six Bells** in St Albans (Roman
treasure); **The Command House** in Chatham (naval ordnance); **Ye Olde
Smugglers Inne** in Alfriston (illegal activities); and **Ye Olde Reindeer** in
Banbury (Cromwell's HQ).

DRINKING TROPHIES

# Pub Crimes

Your nearest branch of Starbucks or Costa Coffee isn't the place to hatch a major crime. Proper villainy begins down the pub. You may not catch Kevin-the-safe-cracker laying out the plans to your nearest Barclays Bank vaults across a load of soggy beermats but the pub is where connections are made and winks are tipped. Some of the most horrible crimes were dreamt up in Britain's pubs, including the plots for most of Guy Ritchie's films.

## 🍾 The Great Train Robbery

**The Star Tavern** in Belgravia was a known haunt in the 1950s and 1960s, not only of many big-league London criminals but of big-screen celebrities such as Diana Dors and Albert Finney. The stars got a kick out of hanging out with London's underworld, and the crooks … well, in 1963, some of them were planning The Great Train Robbery. Bruce Reynolds and Buster Edwards cooked up the scheme here, meeting regularly in the Star with other members of the 15-strong gang. They got away with £2.6 million after stopping a mail train on Sears Crossing in Buckinghamshire. Their most famous member, Ronnie Biggs, eluded capture for many years but finally returned from Brazil to Britain in 2001 at the age of 71 because, he said, he just wanted to "walk into a Margate pub as an Englishman and buy a pint of bitter."

## 🍾 Jack the Ripper

Many Whitechapel pubs claim gruesome connections with Jack the Ripper, the 1888 serial killer whose identity is still the subject of morbid fascination. His victims were prostitutes who found clients at many of the bars in the area. **The Princess Alice** (now called The City Darts) was one such, frequented by Frances Coles, whose death by knifing made her a possible Ripper victim. Another regular was John 'Leather Apron' Pizer, known to hold a knife to prostitutes and threaten to 'rip them up'. He was arrested for the murders but later cleared. The best known Ripper pub is **The Ten Bells**, which even briefly changed its name to **The Jack the Ripper** between 1976 and 1988. Two of his victims are known to have been regulars there – Annie Chapman and Mary Kelly. Mary regarded the pub as her personal pitch which she defended violently against any poachers. The Bells has a rather happier association these days thanks to a former landlord, Jamie Oliver's great great grandfather, who held the tenancy during the 1880s.

##  Skulls: Every Pub Should Have One...

In the early 19th century the East End of London was no stranger to violent death. But the Ratcliffe Highway murders of two hard-working families in 1811 were so frenzied that they shocked the city. Three members of the Marr family were killed in their draper's shop, and two weeks later three members of the Williamson household in their pub, **The King's Arms** on Garnet Street. The chief suspect, John Williams, whose initials were found beneath dried blood and matted hair on one of the murder weapons, never faced trial. He was found hanging in his cell on the morning of the hearing, and buried – as was traditional for suicides – at a crossroads, the meeting of Cable Road and Cannon Street Road opposite **The Crown and Dolphin**. When workers were laying gas pipes there in 1886, they found the body face down with a stake through its heart. They gave the skull to the landlord of The Crown and Dolphin, who displayed it behind his bar. The pub is closed now, and the location of the skull unknown.

## Trains and Boats and Chains

**The Mitford Castle** in Bow, now an Irish theme bar called **The Top O' the Morning**, claims a little piece of railway history as the place where the first victim of assault on board a train died. James Briggs was brought there alive when railway workers found him at the side of the tracks, but he died of his wounds. The attacker, Franz Muller, fled on a slow boat to America, but was pursued by Scotland Yard on a faster steamship. He was arrested in Manhattan, extradited, convicted and hanged outside Newgate Prison in front of 50,000 drunken revellers. You never hear that kind of fact on *Great Railway Journeys* with Michael Portillo.

"A tavern is a place where madness is sold by the bottle."

*Jonathan Swift*

The Blind Beggar dates from 1894 but was
built on the site of a former inn dating to 1654.
The legend of the Blind Beggar is based on
Henry de Montfort (son of Simon) who lost his
sight in the Battle of Evesham in 1265. He ended
up in Bethnal Green begging at the crossroads.

## The Kray Twins

**The Blind Beggar** in Whitechapel has a diverse history. It is the site of the formation of the Salvation Army; William Booth preached his first open-air sermon outside the pub in 1865. The present building dates from 1894, and is more notorious as the bar where London gangster Ronnie Kray shot and killed George Cornell of the rival Richardson gang in 1966. Although the lounge was full of witnesses, not one was prepared to testify against one of the Kray twins. In 1967 Ronnie and Reggie Kray bought their mother a present, **The Carpenter's Arms** in Spitalfields. The bar top, it was rumoured, was made of coffin lids, a macabre touch of humour from the brothers who spent their lives filling coffins. It was from the Carpenters in October that year that the brothers set off with Jack McVitie, a member of their gang, for a basement flat in Clapton, where they violently stabbed him to death with a carving knife. The following year the Krays and most of the gang were arrested, convicted and imprisoned. Ronnie, declared insane, died in Broadmoor in 1995. Reggie, suffering from inoperable cancer, was released on compassionate grounds in August 2000 and died two months later. His cortege paused as it passed The Carpenter's Arms on his final journey. The pub closed in 2005 but re-opened four years later, refurbished and determined to leave its association with London's most ruthless gang firmly in the past. But it still has that bar top ...

> "I have two ambitions in life: one is to drink every pub dry, the other is to sleep with every woman on earth."
>
> *Oliver Reed*

###  The Tide is High but I'm Holding On

A noose hangs in the window of **The Prospect of Whitby** pub in Wapping, as a dubious tribute to hanging judge George Jeffreys, who sentenced to death many of the supporters of Monmouth's Rebellion in 1685. The Prospect, Jeffrey's local, claims to be London's oldest waterside inn, a former smugglers' haunt dating back to 1520. It was originally known as The Pelican and after that The Devil's Tavern. Captured pirates were tied to stakes on the shore in front of the pub at low tide and left to drown. It was rebuilt in the early 19th century after a fire and renamed The Prospect of Whitby, taking the name from a Tyne coal barge of the same name that used to dock alongside.

### The 1381 Peasant's Revolt

**Jack Straw's Castle** was known as London's highest pub until it closed in the 1990s. It sits on the edge of Hampstead Heath, and takes its name from one of the leaders of the 1381 Peasants' Revolt: his 'castle' was the hay wagon from which he stirred up crowds with speeches on the Heath. One of its regulars in the 1850s was the MP John Sadlier whose fraudulent speculation in railway shares brought about the collapse of the Tipperary Bank and the ruin of 4,000 investors. When one night in 1856 he ran out of options to pay his debts, Sadlier mixed a cocktail of prussic acid, opium and sugar in a silver cream jug and drank the poison on the Heath behind the Castle, where he was found dead the following morning.

## The Notorious Dick Turpin

Around two hundred pubs claim a connection with England's most famous highwayman Dick Turpin. Dick's father was a landlord of two of them, both in Hampstead: **The Spaniard's Inn** and **The Bluebell**. The Spaniard's sits opposite a tollbooth and would have made an excellent vantage point. From it you could see which wealthy travellers were using the turnpike road, and how few witnesses there would be to any given highway robbery attempt. When Turpin killed a man who was trying to arrest him, he fled northwards and took rooms at **The Ferry Inn** in Brough on the Humber estuary, adopting a new trade and a new identity – John Palmer, horse thief. When a stolen mare was traced back to him, Dick Turpin was finally captured at The Ferry in 1738. He was hanged in York the following year.

## GBH with a JCB

Perhaps the manager of **The North Star Inn** at Steventon didn't realise, when he refused to serve a drunk who barged in on New Year's Eve 2002, that the customer was also the owner of the pub. Robert Tyrell, the man in question, was so incensed that he went away – and came back driving a mechanical digger, with which he attacked the Grade I listed 16th-century building. The 16 revellers inside, who included his own son, fled for their lives as Tyrell brought down roof and walls with a series of blows. He inflicted £70,000 of damage, but no personal injuries.

## Gunpowder Plot

Britain's most famous act of treason, the Gunpowder Plot, was hatched in **The Duck and Drake Inn** near the Strand in London. There, on 20th May 1604, the five original conspirators including Guy Fawkes met for the first time and made plans to assassinate King James I of England (IV of Scotland) by blowing up the House of Lords during the State Opening of Parliament on 5th November 1605. Like most schemes dreamt up over a drink in a pub, it didn't come off quite as planned.

###  Barclays Get Their Round In

Which of us hasn't wanted to throw £1,200 in banknotes up in the air in a grand gesture? Robin Hood-inspired bank robber Christopher Allnut went straight to the pub with his booty and flung it skywards, announcing, "I've just robbed a bank: the drinks are on me." It was true, as Barclays Bank in Winchester could confirm. Allnut, who was later detained under the Mental Health Act, made the gesture because he knew how poor many of the regulars in the bar were. And the name of the Wetherspoon's pub where he declared his criminal activity? **The Old Gaol House**.

### "You're Getting Warmer…"

Crime hotspot **The North Star** pub in Birkenhead had already had a brush with the law in early 2011 when a cannabis farm was discovered in a rented flat above it. During a further raid on the pub in December, police noticed that the pub was unusually warm, even for the time of year. On closer inspection they discovered a gas meter hanging off the wall in the basement, from which the pub had been syphoning off stolen gas to run its central heating. It emerged that there had been no official gas supply to the pub for five years. The licensee promptly switched to electric heating, but failed to warm the hearts of the licensing committee, who closed the pub down in February 2012.

At the heart of government in Whitehall stands The Silver Cross pub. It still retains its license to run a brothel, first granted by Charles I.

## 🍾 Arson Fire

Arson attacks on pubs are on the increase. Perhaps they're desperate attempts to survive the recession, or maybe they're inspired by the frequency of disastrous fires in pubs on TV soaps. Some are more successful than others. When Michael Morgan wanted revenge after being thrown out of **The Club** in Congleton for fighting in 2011, he returned, drunk, at 5am with a bottle of petrol. In anticipation of a quick getaway he remained on his bicycle as he poured the flammable liquid through the pub's letterbox. The petrol however seeped back out below the door, and as Morgan bent to light it, the whole lot blew up in his face. He pedalled off at speed with his trousers on fire, causing minimal damage to The Club.

## 🎯 The Smuggler's Rest

Calling a pub The Smuggler's Inn is a bit like calling it The Crackdealer's Arms today. If it were true, you just wouldn't advertise the fact. **Ye Olde Smuggler's Inn** at Alfriston in Essex used to be called **Market Cross House** – and smugglers really did meet there in the 18th century. As well as the usual fabled escape tunnels, the house also had six staircases and 48 doors, a labyrinth with which the smugglers would be familiar but any unwanted visitors from the Inland Revenue would not.

While builders were converting a waterfront warehouse in Penzance in 2008, they stumbled across secret entrances to a network of smugglers' tunnels that led uphill to the **Admiral Benbow** pub, which in the 19th century had its own gang of smugglers – the Benbow Brandy Men.

During renovation work in 1911, workers in the Haunch of Venison pub in Salisbury found a well-preserved severed hand in a wall cavity, along with some 18th-century playing cards.

> "No, Sir, there is nothing which has yet been
> contrived by man, by which so much happiness
> is produced as by a good tavern or inn."
>
> *Samuel Johnson*

##  Shaft – Can Ya Dig It?

Customs men searching for smuggled goods in Witham's 16th-century
**Spread Eagle** were unlikely to find any. The pub has a concealed shaft built
into its walls with no entrance at all from within the building. Smugglers
hoisted their booty onto the roof and lowered it into the hidden space
through a gap in the tiles.

##  And That's Just for Starters...

Our romantic modern view of smugglers overlooks the fact that they
were ruthless, violent gangs of men. A customs officer attempting to arrest
a smuggler in the 16th-century **Black Dog Inn** at Weymouth was murdered
there. Elsewhere, one gruesome report describes the prolonged torture and
murder in 1748 of a customs man and a smuggler turned informant. They
were captured by the notoriously brutal Hawkhurst gang in the **White
Hart Inn** at Rowland's Castle (now demolished). The gang tied them to
their horses and beat them sadistically all the way to the **Red Lion** at Rake,
15 miles away, where one was thrown down a well and the other buried
alive. Even the dead men's horses were killed and flayed to conceal any
evidence that the victims had been there.

## 🍾 What the Dickens?

Workers digging the Gravesend to Strood canal in 1800 fell into one of several smugglers' tunnels radiating out from **The Ship and Lobster** at Gravesend. Charles Dickens mentions the pub's smuggling history in *Great Expectations*. Elsewhere in Gravesend **The Three Daws** pub, Kent's oldest, was built with seven staircases, to give smugglers fleeing a customs raid as many escape routes as possible.

## 🔑 "You're Getting Warmer" II

**The Vigo Inn** on the road from Gravesend to London has a secret chamber hidden behind the fireplace. Smugglers often constructed such places of concealment, reasoning that few revenue officers would try to look beyond a roaring fire in the hearth. **The Ship Inn** at Levington near Ipswich had a hidden cupboard built into the eaves, above the eyeline of most customs officials, who would be looking for trapdoors to concealed cellars beneath their feet.

PUB FACT

When builders were working on the 18th-century Vine Inn at Skegness in 1902, they uncovered the skeleton of a man in uniform, his brass buttons decorated with royal insignia. He was an excise man, last seen entering the Vine in the early 19th century.

# Pub Names

When King Edgar I limited them to one per village they were simply known as 'the pub'. But times changed, villages grew and taverns multiplied. They needed a more marketable brand than 'the other pub'. Richard II brought in the law that each pub should erect a sign so that his ale inspectors could identify taverns and make sure that the ale they served was of the utmost quality. Often pubs didn't have a formal name, they just went by the rudimentary drawing on the sign outside and gradually became known by that image. Surprisingly, no Stickman Inns survive.

## 🍾 Adam and Eve

Biblical names for pubs are often an indicator that they are very old. Many inns sprang up and prospered on the routes to Britain's holiest places, such as York Minster, Ripon, Glastonbury and Canterbury. Having biblical characters, angels or saints on the pub sign was a surefire way to cash in on the booming pilgrimage trade.

## 🎻 Angel

Many inns and taverns started off in life with religious names because they were sited on land owned by the church. When protestant Parliamentarian Oliver Cromwell seized power any name linked to Catholicism, particularly the veneration of Mary, was cast into the wilderness. Straightforward biblical names were fine, so taverns such as the Adam and Eve, Rainbow & Dove, Good Samaritan, David and Goliath could continue. There were also pubs called the Salutation with an image of the Archangel Gabriel welcoming the Virgin Mary on their signs. To appease the new pub puritans, tavern owners removed Mary and so their pubs duly became The Angel.

PUB FACT

There are still some 70 different saints mentioned in the names of British pubs, the most common one being St George, as in The George and Dragon.

 **Bag O' Nails**

One step up from the Blacksmiths Arms, the Bag O' Nails is a pub for ironmongers. Although some pub historians think it might be a corruption of the Roman festival of drunken rowdiness *Bacchanalia*. (Also a form of insult aimed at women, "I wouldn't say she was ugly but she's got a face like a bacchanalia.")

**Barley Mow**

Mow might be a verb, as in mowing the grass, but applied to a pub sign the 'mow' is a barley stack or rick made up of the sheaves of barley gathered from the field. As the principal ingredients of beer are barley and water it's an unsurprising name for a pub. And you can add to that The Maltster's Arms, the John Barleycorn and the J. D. Wetherspoons.

**Bear and Ragged Staff**

Similar to the country sign of Warwickshire, the heraldic image of a bear with a ragged staff is the coat of arms of the Earls of Warwick, the Neville family. In Arthurian times one of the family supposedly made a name for himself by strangling a bear with his bare hands (or his bear hands). Quite a few more heraldic emblems have made their way into publore.

**Bell**

At the core of any village are its church and its pub. They are never far away from each other and the proximity of the two institutions and their twin approaches to claim mortal souls have been the subject of charming witticisms in *Reader's Digest* over the years. A lot of pubs are called the Bell because when pub signs were quite primitive, things like bells, moons, stars and crowns were easy to draw and recognize. Often when a pub is called the Seven Bells or Eight Bells that refers to the number of bells in the nearby church.

**Black Dog**

Legends abound about black dogs in English folklore, and we're not talking about the affable, short-haired black retriever. Traditional black dogs are devil dogs or hellhounds that appear in the night to scare the livin' bejesus out of ye. Pub signs may have beautified them over the years, but they started off as fearful creatures known through the counties by a variety of local names: the Barghest of Yorkshire, the Black Shuck of East Anglia, Hairy Jack, Padfoot, Churchyard Beast, Shug Monkey, Galleytrot,

Capelthwaite, Mauthe Doog, Bogey Beast (Lancashire), Gytrash and Gurt Dog. Somerset's great dog or Gurt Dog is more like Peter Pan's 'Nana' and the tales go that mothers would let their children play unsupervised in the Quantock Hills because they believed that the Gurt Dog would protect them. These days that's not enough for Social Services.

The spiritual home of pub rock is The Hope and Anchor in Islington which has hosted Dire Straits, U2, XTC, The Police, The Stranglers, Keane and Dr Feelgood. It was also the venue for the Stranglers' double album, 'Live at the Hope and Anchor' recorded in 1977.

## Black Horse

Putting a fine black horse on a pub sign in the 18th and 19th century would be the equivalent of putting a Lamborghini Murcielago or Aston Martin Vanquish on there today. Pubs and inns were named the Black Horse for aesthetic reasons and also because they offered stabling. (And, ironically, cash loans.)

## Blue Boar

As with The Bear and Ragged Staff, many pub names evolved from heraldic crests – and sometimes just elements of them. Long since hunted into extinction, 'blue' boars were symbolized in the coat of arms for the earls of Oxford and thus many occur where they held land and influence. In the same way, the White Hart was part of Richard II's coat of arms and the Red Lion part of John of Gaunt's. The Hanoverian kings were distinguished by their heraldic representation of a White Horse.

## Bombay Grab

A once-famous pub on the Bow Road in East London, the Bombay Grab should probably have been called the Bombay Gurab (gurab is the Arabic word for a two-masted Eastern sailing vessel). It was built by East London brewers Hodgson's who were doing a roaring trade supplying beer to the British Empire in the early 19th century, especially to the East India Company's Bombay HQ. By 1815 they were supplying 4,000 barrels a year from their brewery by Bow Bridge and the Grab was the brewery's own public house nearby. It closed in 1992 and with a rich irony is now used as a mosque and Muslim cultural centre.

## Britannia

When the Romans invaded the British Isles they didn't bother with Ireland (Hibernia), struggled with those north of Hadrian's Wall (Caledonia) but attempted to convert the rest (Britannia) to their way of life. As part of the process of keeping the rebellious Brits onside they took a Celtic goddess, Brigantia, and gave her a Roman makeover, complete with flowing robe and centurion's helmet. The figure of Britannia was largely forgotten during the dark and middle ages but was resurrected as a means of uniting the people in the early 18th century. And the naming of pubs followed.

## The Bull

Ambridge's favourite pub – were it real – could have had a couple of possible explanations for its name. While the bull has long been an essential part of the rural economy (and some feminists might say 'part of our phallocentric society' – you don't get pubs named the Dairy Cow or the Suckling Ewe; you get Bull, Ram, Cock and Boar), naming your tavern The Bull could also be seen as a nod to Catholic sentiments. Edicts from the Pope came in the form of papal bulls (named after the papal seal). Once Henry VIII decided to cut his ties with Rome he adopted a severed bull's head as part of his coat of arms. And so naming your tavern the Bull's Head could be seen as backing royalty.

> "When you have lost your inns, drown your empty selves, for you will have lost the last of England."
>
> *Hillaire Belloc*

56

## Bush

Back in Anglo Saxon days each village had its own brewer, but presumably because he or she had to go off serfing for the Lord of the Manor, they couldn't be doing it full time. So, to let the rest of the villagers know whenever there was a brew ready they would stick a bush outside the house – sometimes a bush with berries for flavouring the beer, as hops had yet to become an ingredient. Such was the popularity of public houses that by 965 King Edgar had to issue an edict limiting them to one per village. Shepherd's Bush in West London, which was rural land right up to the 1840s, is thought to be named after the shepherd's alehouse.

## Cat and Fiddle

There are some ingenious explanations as to why you should have a pub named after a nursery rhyme, as in: *Hey diddle diddle, the cat and the fiddle, the cow jumped over the moon*. Some have put forward the cumbersome theory that the name is a corruption of the French for 'faithful cat' which is *chat fidele*. Others think it's derived from Henry VIII's much-admired first queen, Catherine of Aragon otherwise known as Catherine La Fidele. But most likely it is derived from the nursery rhyme. Although the rhyme is only seen in print from the mid-18th century there were Cat and Fiddles in London almost two centuries before and no doubt the rhyme had been passed down over the generations with no need to write something so trifling on a piece of valuable paper. There are many nursery rhyme pub signs: Jack and Jill, Little Jack Horner, Simple Simon, Cock Robin, Mother Hubbard, The Man in the Moon etc.

## Chequers

The chequerboard dates back to Roman times and examples of it were found in ancient Pompei. Its association with pubs goes back to the time when you could go down to the pub to borrow money. In 15th-century Oxford, The Chequers Inn shared its courtyard with a moneylender and this seems to have been a widespread practice. Sometimes the landlords themselves were moneylenders, putting far more than a night's worth of drinks on the slate.

## Coach and Horses

Before the railways came, Britain was connected by coaching roads and given the state of the roads – mud, rocks, fallen-trees, contra-flows – journeys were long. For the coach driver with limited lateral thinking, the Coach and Horses was the perfect name to attract trade; it did what it said on the tin – a bit like that old restaurant chain Happy Eater. Charles Dickens was both a prolific pubgoer, traveller and a prodigious pub incorporator and used a real-life **Coach and Horses** (in London Road, Isleworth) in *Oliver Twist*:

> *As they passed the different mile-stones, Oliver wondered, more and more, where his companion meant to take him. Kensington, Hammersmith, Chiswick, Kew Bridge, Brentford, were all passed; and yet they went on as steadily as if they had only just begun their journey. At length, they came to a public-house called the Coach and Horses; a little way beyond which, another road appeared to run off. And here, the cart stopped.*

## Cock

Struggling to attract custom before the invention of Sky Sports, taverns in the middle ages would often have a cock-fighting pit. Cockerels were part of the village scene – workers had to be up at daylight and so they were the radio/alarm of the rural economy. Out in the village they could strut around and keep their distance from other aggressive cocks, but in a confined space they were up for it. The pits didn't need to be particularly big, hence the derivation of the word cockpit for an aircraft. Thus there are many pubs still called the Cock and the Fighting Cocks.

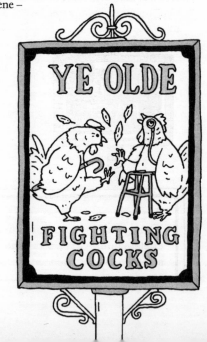

**Cross Keys**

A pub name with a firmly religious connection, the crossed keys are the sign of St. Peter who stands at the entrance to heaven waiting to unlock his pearly gates. Or not, if that person was always disappearing to the toilet when it was their round. It's not known why you would need a solid key to open up an abstract concept – but obviously you needed at least one and a spare.

**Dick Turpin**

There are a few Dick Turpin pubs around and his stature as a noble and gentlemanly highwayman is based more on the highly romanticised version of Turpin's life by Harrison Ainsworth (1834) than anything else. Adam Ant's version was probably just as close to the truth. The son of an innkeeper from Hempstead in Essex, he turned to highway robbery after most of the burglary gang he was a member of had been hanged or transported. He was as much a horse thief as a highway robber and was ultimately caught and hanged in York in 1739. There was no heroic ride to York on Black Bess either – although highwayman 'Swift' Nick Nevison was said to have tried that particular ruse to create an alibi in 1684.

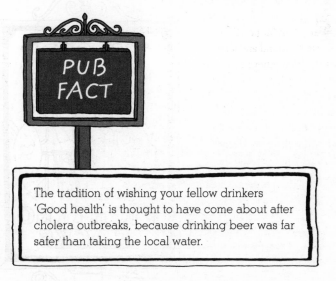

PUB
FACT

The tradition of wishing your fellow drinkers 'Good health' is thought to have come about after cholera outbreaks, because drinking beer was far safer than taking the local water.

## 🛢 Dog and...

There are a host of country inns that reference hunting in their name, most obviously The Dog and Fox and The Fox and Hounds. The inn was often located close to the village green where the huntsmen and women could gather on horseback for a stirrup cup before tallying ho off into the countryside and ripping apart many beautiful country hedges and the occasional inadvertent fox. There are also pubs named the Dog and Duck, for those shooting wildfowl and the Dog and Bear, from a time when bear baiting was seen as entertainment and there is the even-less-sporting Dog and Hedgehog.

## 🍾 Druid's Arms / Druid's Head

As any average student of history will know, ancient druids were too busy sacrificing animals, growing beards and re-arranging stones to bother about brewing beer. The naming of various pubs for druids – more often than not miles from any ancient stone circles is likely to be thanks to a benevolent society known as the Ancient Order of Druids founded in the 1780s or its extreme wing, the United Ancient Order of Druids. They would meet in pubs and hotels and discuss good deeds, very much like the Lions Club but with Druid fundamentalist beards.

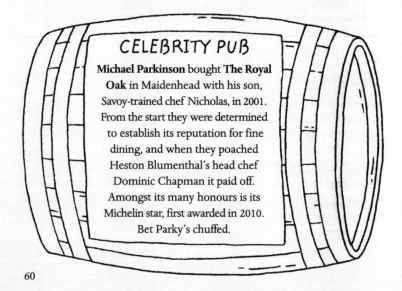

### CELEBRITY PUB

**Michael Parkinson** bought **The Royal Oak** in Maidenhead with his son, Savoy-trained chef Nicholas, in 2001. From the start they were determined to establish its reputation for fine dining, and when they poached Heston Blumenthal's head chef Dominic Chapman it paid off. Amongst its many honours is its Michelin star, first awarded in 2010. Bet Parky's chuffed.

## Duke's Head

Britain was always involved in some war or another through its history, and pubs were often named after a war hero. Thus the latest hero might be the Duke of Wellington, or it could be the Duke of York or the Duke of Cumberland. The easiest way to capitalise on the latest heroic military Duke would be to call your pub the Duke's Head and change the pub sign to fit whoever was in favour with the public.

## Dun Cow

Imagine a terrifyingly big cow roaming the fields of Warwickshire with red eyes ablaze. Imagine also a formerly sweet-natured cow with an endless supply of milk who would happily give up a pail of her finest to anyone who would set up a stool at her gigantic udders. The change from gentle farm beast to cow-zilla came when the cow was taunted by a woman who milked her into a sieve. The Dun Cow ran dry and cow-mageddon ensued; a state of affairs that was finally put to rest when Guy of Warwick (who sounds less like a knight and more like a gents' outfitters) slayed the animal. Pubs were named to commemorate the event.

## Eagle and Child

The most famous Eagle and Child pub is in Oxford and was frequented by a writers' group that included J.R.R. Tolkien and C.S. Lewis, and presumably other authors who didn't want their first names widely known. Tolkien would have appreciated the story behind the pub name, taken from the Lathom and Stanley families' crest of an eagle and child. Back in the 14th century Sir Thomas Lathom was only able to sire daughters and in those days it was the woman's fault. Which is perhaps why he thought his wife might be open to a far-fetched suggestion. So desperate was he to have a male heir that he got his newly born illegitimate son placed underneath a tree where eagles nested. 'Chancing' upon it with his wife, he noted that providence, in the form of an eagle, had brought him a son and they should adopt it. He was rumbled in the end.

### Elephant and Castle

The pub in Newington which gave the name Elephant and Castle to an area of South London is long gone. It was sited on a former blacksmith's forge that also carried that name thanks to its connection to the Worshipful Company of Cutlers, a venerable trade guild dating back to medieval times. Their coat of arms had elephants equipped with small towers, or *howdahs*, similar to the ones used in Julius Caesar's Games of 46 BC. The blacksmith had a sign boasting of its connection to such an esteemed body (in those days cutlers also made weapons) which was taken on by the pub and then taken on by the district. Although there are many stories that link the pub to Edward I's wife Eleanor, the Infanta de Castile (or Eleanor of Castile), no link has ever been proven.

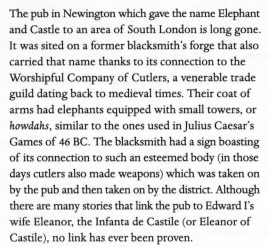

### Foresters Arms

The Foresters and Foresters' Arms pubs were named after benevolent societies set up to look after the interests of forestry workers. These included the Royal Order of Foresters and the Ancient Order of Foresters. In the past, forestry was a tough job – apart from looking after the trees foresters often had to deal with wandering bands of dangerous vagrants who would roam around and hide out in the woods for days on end. Or ramblers as they were often known.

### Frozen Mop

Although local byelaws are supposed to govern these things, opening hours have often been subject to the whim of the landlord. At the Weavers Arms in Bolton the landlady was a fearsome character not to be messed with. She opened when it suited her and to signal that the pub was open for business she would leave a mop outside. For that reason the pub became known locally as T'Frizzen Mop (the Frozen Mop). There is also a Frozen Mop in Mobberley, near Knutsford in Cheshire.

### George

Named after the elector of Hanover, George I put England on the road to a solid Protestant future and firmly established a constitutional monarchy. Having been through the uncertainties of James I, and then William and Mary, England finally had a stable government not undermined by the king. Everybody could breathe a sigh of relief and go down the pub. Calling your pub The George was both a patriotic duty and a moneyspinner.

## George and Dragon

England's patron saint was a Christian soldier martyred in AD 303 fighting in Palestine. He was less of a 'good-deeds saint' or a 'rags-and-poverty saint' and more of an 'action-hero saint'. Saint George acted as an inspiration to Richard the Lionheart and the crusaders to fight the fiendish Saracens in the Holy Land. The Feast of St George, on April 23rd, was introduced as early as 1222. During the Reformation people were only allowed to celebrate saints mentioned in the bible, but George was already too firmly established in the public mind to be banished. The dragon element was introduced to sex up the story. It's widely thought that the tale of George rescuing a fair maiden was adapted from the Greek story of *Perseus and Andromeda*.

## Green Man

Originally the Green Man was a representation of a large pagan man covered in leaves and swishing a large club. Fashions changed and in the 19th century many of the wild green men were replaced by figures such as Robin Hood, or those who made their living dressed in green such as foresters or gamekeepers. Since then the pendulum has swung back to show more folkloric type green men and also what's known as a 'foliate head', a face that is sprouting leaves. Examples are found in many medieval churches and are thought to embody the spirit of new growth and fertility.

## Hobgoblin

Named after one of Wychwood's brewery's most famous ales, Hobgoblin, the name comes from the same root as the Hobbit – also the name of a pub – hob. Tolkien took this country name for a mischievous elfin creature and created his own world, but the terminology for both is centuries old. They are included in a list of local fairies, spirits and bogies compiled by Victorian writer Michael Denham, including hob, hobbit, hobgoblin, hobthrust and hobman. Hob was the shortened name for Robin or Robert and in Shakespeare's *A Midsummer Night's Dream*, the mischievous Puck's alternative name is Robin Goodfellow. "Those that hobgoblin call you, and sweet Puck…"

## Hope and Anchor

A pub named with pious intent; Faith, Hope and Charity are the three cardinal virtues – but one virtue is probably enough for a pub. Saint Paul referred to hope as 'a sure and steadfast anchor of the soul'. Many of the bands playing in North London's hallowed pub rock venue of the same name were certainly hoping for more than "£25 a night and bring your own P.A.".

## Horseshoe

An upturned horseshoe brings good luck, and half the reason is because they act as a handy witch repellent. Since medieval times, iron has been the go-to material for repelling supernatural evil and an upturned horseshoe nailed to the front door will guarantee the owner a witch-free future. Thus the sight of one, three, or even four horseshoes on a pub sign bodes well if you want an evening of witch-free drinking.

## John Bull

History shows us that almost everything was invented in Scotland or by Scots: the television, the telephone, penicillin and, it turns out, John Bull. The creation of political satirist John Arbuthnot, John Bull was the archetypal "honest, bold, plain-dealing" Englishman up against his double-crossing enemies, the Dutch 'Nick Frog' and the French 'Louis Baboon'. If Al Murray – the pub landlord – ever became a publican in real-life, this would surely be his chosen pub name.

## King's Head

Celebrating the monarch at the time, if the pub sign is of Charles I, then it literally is the king's head.

## Lamb and Flag

Drawn from religious art – the lamb represents the re-born, resurrected Jesus holding up a banner that represents his victory over death and his persecutors. This traditional symbolism was also used in heraldry and crests of the ancient trade guilds.

## Man in the Moon

With no entertainment industry to speak of in the middle ages, villagers had to amuse themselves of an evening by staring at the moon. Those who stared long enough were convinced that they saw a man carrying a bundle of sticks and holding a lantern. Thus the legend was born, which Shakespeare worked into *A Midsummer Night's Dream*, and which Noel Fielding and Julian Barratt latterly used in *The Mighty Boosh*, though without the sticks.

PUB FACT

In Butlin's holiday camps there was a variety of bars, including the Hawaiian Bar, the Gaiety Bar, the Crazy Horse Saloon bar, but their mock-Tudor, half-timbered pubs were called The Pig and Whistle.

## Marquis of Granby

A daring cavalry officer in the Seven Years' War against the French, John Manners led a charge at the Battle of Warburg which resulted in a much-needed victory for the British. He was popular with the public and also with his men, a trait that was criticised by those who didn't like officers fraternising with the ranks. But like many war heroes, the qualities that served him well on the battlefield couldn't be carried over into peace time, yet it was said that he continued to take an interest in the soldiers who had served him, setting up many of them as innkeepers, who returned the favour by naming their taverns in his honour.

## Maypole

Villages from Tudor times would cut down a tall, straight tree, lop off the branches and paint it to create their very own maypole. This was then erected in a communal place where much traditional roistering could take place. In past times it was flower garlands and greenery that decorated the pole. From the 1830s, brightly coloured ribbons would be attached to the pole around which the children of the village could dance on May Day – and do all the kind of activities that filled 34 series of *Lark Rise to Candleford*. Maypole pubs are found throughout the country, including Surbiton, on a lane reputedly used by Henry VIII nipping between Hampton Court and Nonsuch Palace.

## Mermaid

A pub name usually – but not exclusively – linked to coastal locations. The two most famous Mermaids are the historic inn in Mermaid Street, Rye, once the hangout of the notorious smuggling Hawkhurst Gang who would sit in the window looking out onto Mermaid Street and carouse (something only pirates and smugglers do) with their loaded pistols on the table. The other being Shakespeare's local in Cheapside, London, burnt down in the Great Fire of London and not far from the Mermaid Theatre. Mermaids supposedly lure sailors to their death, but in Leek, in Staffordshire, the Mermaid Inn is close to the bottomless Mermaid's Pool of Blackshaw Moor.

In this place a mermaid would casually hoik in and drown passers-by if they strayed too close after midnight (or most likely staggered in after a skinfull).

## Nag's Head

A pub with a sign showing a horse's head was a good indicator that you could hire a horse there. The Nag's Head could also differentiate between clientele by having the pub regulars in the Head and the rowdy, lute-, piano-, banjo- or jukebox-playing young crowd in the Nag's Tail. Occasionally, the pub sign is a variant of that used for pubs such as The Quiet Woman, The Silent Woman or The Good Woman (pictured above).

## Phoenix

Symbolizing a rejuvenation after disaster, the Phoenix bird lives for 500 years, then lays a single egg and bursts into flames. The warmth from the flames helps the solitary egg hatch and a new phoenix bird rises from the ashes giving the phrase 'phoenix from the flames'.

## Pig and Whistle

Many theories abound about how this pub name came about – some think it relates to the fact that beer was held in large barrels or 'pigs' down in the cellar. While the potboys were filling up the pots and tankards out of sight they were required to whistle to prove they weren't just drinking the beer. Another centres around a corruption of the word 'wassail' – spiced ail or cider, served with a spitroasted hog. The most likely root is the phrase 'to go to pigs and whistles' which means to go to rack and ruin, something that can be associated with spending large amounts of time down the pub. Or... the landlord just liked the picture of a pig with a penny whistle.

## Plough

Catering to rural workers, the Plough is one of many agricultural names to make it onto pub signs. Variants include The Plough and Harrow, Plough and Horses, Plough and Sail (with the sail being that fixed to a windmill) and Speed the Plough. In addition to the livestock names mentioned earlier (Bull, Ram, Boar, Cock), there's the Wheatsheaf, the Barley Sheaf, the Barley Mow, the Harvester, the Farmer's Boy and not forgetting the Jolly Farmer – a contradiction if ever there was one. But then the name 'Miserable Pessimist Farmer' is never going to be a big crowd-puller.

## Red Lion

John of Gaunt was the third son of Edward III and married the Infanta Constance of Castile. It was a political match and he incorporated the red lion from her family crest into his own coat of arms. In 1386 he left the young and increasingly unpopular Richard II (he's the one that sent out the ale inspectors in 1393) to govern the country while he went off to claim the throne of Castile. John had a legitimate claim to the throne himself and so inns and taverns that supported him would display the red lion. In response, Richard II ruled that taverns should bear his own crest, the white hart. On Gaunt's return to England he threw his weight behind Richard II who was eventually forced out by Gaunt's son, Henry Bolingbroke who became Henry IV.

## Rising Sun

Another heraldic image – the symbol of a sun rising has been used in royal coats of arms since the time of Edward III. Most pubs of this name are in the UK, but there is a house in New Orleans...

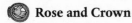 **Rose and Crown**

The Rose and Crown represents the end of the Wars of the Roses, when Henry Tudor triumphed over Richard III (a.k.a. The King in the Car Park) at the Battle of Bosworth and swiftly married Elizabeth of York to unite the House of Lancaster with the House of York. Instead of displaying a red rose or a white rose, tavern landlords could now depict the red-and-white Tudor rose and sleep easy.

### Royal Oak

After Charles II was defeated by Oliver Cromwell at the Battle of Worcester, he was legging it to safety with the Parliamentarians hot on his heels. Close to the Shropshire/Staffordshire border, at Boscobel, he climbed into a tree with Charles Giffard and spent the day watching the Roundheads search property and woodland nearby. Nine years later he returned in triumph for the restoration and his birthday, 29th May, which became Oak Apple Day – a national celebration that lasted 200 years. Pubs and inns followed.

### Saracen's Head / Turk's Head

Rooted in the Crusades, noble families who fought in the wars to evict the Saracens from the Holy Land would add a Saracen's head to the family crest, to show they fought the good fight. These, like many heraldic images, found their way onto pub signs.

### Star and Garter

Edward III's influence on heraldry indirectly helped name a lot of British pubs – and it was Ed who instigated the Order of the Garter for his 24 top knights. Charles I added an eight-point star to the award making it the Royal Star and Garter.

## Swan, White Swan, Black Swan, Swan with Two Nicks

The swan has been designated a royal bird since the 12th century, and so this most graceful of creatures has adorned pub signs mostly by rivers (Thames Ditton, Upton-upon-Severn) and occasionally by lakes and ponds (Hanley Swan). You can have White Swans (Richmond, Bosham) and Black Swans (Alderley Edge) and then there are the Swans with Two Nicks. Queen Elizabeth I broadened out swan ownership in the 16th century, allowing the Worshipful Company of Vintners and also the Dyers a bit of Swan-upmanship. The swan-uppers would leave the Queen's swans unmarked but would put one nick on the beak of a Dyer swan, and two on a Vintner swan – hence there are a lot more pubs named The Swan with Two Nicks (Worcester) than one nick.

**PUB FACT**

The pub name Pig and Whistle gives rise to one of the longest consecutive uses of the word 'and' in a sentence. A signwriter goes to write the name of The Pig and Whistle above the door of the pub, but the landlord is not happy about the spacing of the words. He says: "there's too much space between 'pig' and 'and' and 'and' and 'whistle'."

## Three...

There are a number of pubs that begin with the word Three – Three Arrows (Guild of Fletchers), Three Crowns (James I uniting Scotland, England and Ireland), Three Feathers (Prince of Wales), Three Horseshoes (near a blacksmith), Three-Legged Mare (gallows humour, it is actually the slang name for a gallows), Three Nuns, Three Tuns (largest wine cask holding 256 gallons), Three Witches (in Stratford-upon-Avon, from *Macbeth*) and the Three Kings. The Three Kings were the Magi, or three wise men, who followed the star to Bethlehem. One of the greatest small pub survivors is the Three Kings at Hanley Castle, near Upton-upon-Severn in Worcestershire. Ironically, it was named after the three Kings brothers who owned the pub in the late 17th century, but it's the Magi who make it onto the sign.

## Volunteer

Pubs in the major ports had long been good places for the notorious press gangs to operate. From 1664 the Royal Navy had been allowed to forcibly 'impress' new recruits. They had to be "eligible men of seafaring habits between the ages of 18 and 45 years". And to use a good nautical term, if they were already 'three sheets to the wind' it was much easier to impress them. By the time of the Franco-Austrian war, the army was also short of men but rather than forcing them to join, they set up volunteer posts in taverns and inns – always a good place for a fight. Soon the army had 170,000 pubs and a few more inns called The Volunteer.

## White Hart

A hart is a male deer and the white hart is a beast that Sir Gawain went chasing after in the legends of King Arthur. It was the heraldic symbol of Richard II and it was as well to keep on his good side by displaying the sign of the hart, as he was the man responsible for crushing the poll tax riots of 1381. There are many White Harts still, but the most famous gave its name to a lane and thus a football ground in North London.

## White Lion

Unlike the disliked Richard II, the much-liked Edward IV had a white lion on his shield. Barbary lions from north-west Africa – the largest species of lion and the ones that Rome imported for gladiatorial fights – were believed to have been imported for a royal menagerie at the Tower of London during his reign.

## Woolpack

With its rolling temperate acres, England was the perfect home for sheep in the middle ages and wool became the country's No.1 export. A woolpack is a bale of wool ready to be sent to mill. So important was the industry that Edward I decided to standardize the woolpack at 240 lb. The most famous Woolpack is in TV soap *Emmerdale*, although the very first was the victim of subsidence, caused by the TV company wanting to switch locations.

## World's End

There are many interpretations of the World's End in pub signs. Some place it at the edge of a flat planet, beyond which the world just stopped and which Vikings would cheerfully sail over the edge. Some use the sign as the portent of some cataclysmic disaster, such as the ones prophesized by Old Mother Shipton or Nostradamus. In Edinburgh they take a more parochial view; that civilization lies within the old city and the world ends beyond the Flodden Wall over which the World's End pub was built. This is true for eleven months of the year, the only exception being August when civilisation leaves town and the world's drama students arrive.

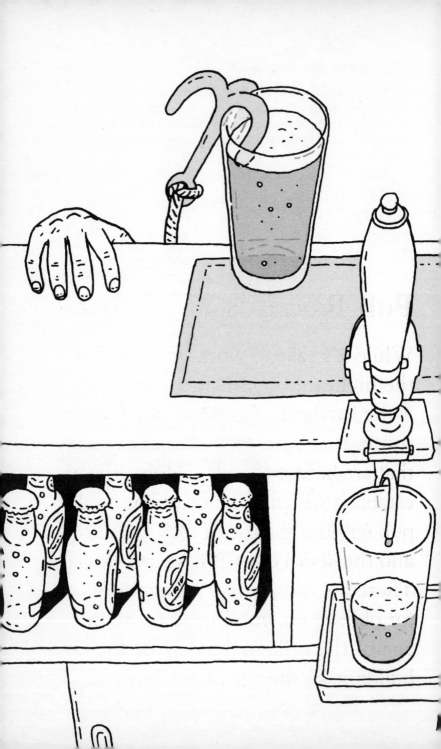

# Pub Records

While it's easy to work out which is the highest pub in Britain, or which is the furthest east, west, north and south, there are many benchmarks that are harder to judge. How do you establish which is the most haunted pub without the use of Orb Detectors and the services of Bill Murray? There are quite a few contenders for oldest pub, but do you go by the age of the cellars, the date of the building, or the age of the carpet...?

## Highest

**The Tan Hill Inn** in Yorkshire, famous for double glazing adverts and snowbound lock-ins, is the highest pub in Britain at 1,732 ft. In Wales the honour belonged to **The Sportsman's Arms** in Bylchau, about 1,440 ft up, until 2012 when it closed. Its rival at 1,390 ft, **The Lamb and Fox** above Blaenavon, now holds the crown. The highest in Scotland is **The Wanlockhead Inn**, 1,531 ft above sea level, where the village also provides something to do while you're drinking – it boasts the second oldest subscription library in Europe.

## Smallest

There are several contenders for Britain's smallest pub including **The Hole in the Wall**, Brighton, but *The Guinness Book of World Records* recognises **The Nutshell** in Bury St Edmunds, which measures up at just 16 ft 6 in by 6 ft 6 in and can hold around a dozen drinkers. In 1984, heedless of health and safety, they squeezed 102 customers into the place for a bet. The smallest bar within a pub is in **The Dove** in London – 7ft 10 in by 4 ft 2 in.

PUB FACT

In 2012 it was reported that pubs were closing at the rate of 18 every week, up from 12 a week the previous year. In 1980 there were 70,000 pubs in the UK; in 2013 there were less than 50,000.

**Largest**

The largest pub in Britain, and possibly in Europe, is **The Moon Under Water**, Manchester. This former cinema, now part of the Wetherspoon's chain, has a capacity of 1,700. The name comes from an essay by George Orwell in which he describes his ideal pub (see page 102), although he doesn't suggest one with quite such a large capacity.

## Oldest

The oldest pubs are older than most castles. **Ye Olde Trip to Jerusalem** in Nottingham is known to have existed at least as long ago as 1189. **The Ostrich** in Colnbrook claims roots going back to 1106. **Ye Olde Fighting Cocks** in St Albans gets the nod in *The Guinness Book of World Records* because its foundations date from 793. But the Cocks' claim is disputed because its timber frame was dismantled and rebuilt in 1485 a few yards to the left of its original location. Because of their tendency to burn down through history, many old pubs have cellars that are even older, sometimes as old as the selection of bar snacks.

## Most Haunted

It's a crowded field in the competition for most haunted pub. Amongst the regular front runners is **The Bucket of Blood** at Hayle in Cornwall, so named because once a landlord drew a pail of blood from his well and discovered the body of a revenue inspector at the bottom of the shaft. Many sightings and spooky sounds have followed. A 17th-century landlord of **The Ostrich Inn** in Colnbrook supposedly murdered more than 60 guests in their beds by dropping them through a trapdoor into a vat of boiling water. (Anything to avoid a poor Trip Advisor rating.) Despite that, the guests often return. **The Red Lion** at Avebury sits on an intersection of ley lines at the centre of one of the finest stone circles in England, and Florrie a former landlady murdered by her husband for infidelity, still appears. So too do a bearded man, a spinning chandelier and a coach and horses, the latter either seen or heard but never both.

### Most Remote

The most remote pub in Britain is **The Old Forge** on the Knoydart peninsula in western Scotland. There are no roads to it. On a good day it's a seven-mile passenger ferry crossing from Mallaig; on a bad day it's an 18-mile hike overland.

### Most Disorientating: The Leaning Pub of Himley

**The Glynne Arms** in Himley, Staffordshire – a.k.a. **The Crooked House** – is surely Britain's most disorientating pub (in a geometric sense). Built over old mine workings, the whole building now lists at an angle of 15 degrees. Negotiating doorways is difficult, even when sober, and the crazy angles of the interior challenge the perceptions of the most modest tippler.

## Longest and Shortest Names

Stalybridge near Manchester has a 'double claim to pub fame' as the home not only of the shortest-named pub in Britain, the succinct and orderly **Q**, but also to the longest – **The Old Thirteenth Cheshire Astley Volunteer Rifleman Corps Inn**. The latter, which opened in 1855 as the rather snappier **New Inn**, became **The Thirteenth Mounted Cheshire Rifleman Inn** before the end of the 19th century. It lost its crown as longest name on a couple of occasions in the 1970s and 1980s, but like any good soldier it rallied to the fight, adding whatever words were necessary to regain the title. Q, by the way, stands for Quirky. Its place in the record books seems unassailable. There was **The Pub With No Name** in Brighton (until renamed **The Southover** in 2013). But although no name is certainly shorter than even a one-letter name, technically The Pub With No Name is, in fact, a name, and a sixteen-letter one at that.

## Flipping Heck

During Proud of Pubs Week in 2010, Dean Gould was at it again, breaking beermat records. On 26th July in **The Wiremill** pub in Lingfield, Surrey he flipped 800 beermats in a record-breaking 41 seconds. In retrospect this was an off-day for Dean, who has since flipped 1,000 mats in 34 seconds. He holds the record in an astounding 13 different beermat categories, including Most in 60 Seconds (2,200), Most at Once (208, interlocked in three piles) and Most Flipped off an Elbow with Palm Up (402 in a single stack). He's versatile – he also holds flipping records for pancakes, coins, Jenga bricks, CDs and 4.5 lb bricks (12 in 11.52 seconds, since you ask). But beermats are his first love, ever since his first successful attempt, in **The Feathers** pub in his native Felixstowe. There, on 16th March 1987, he flipped 65 mats, two at a time, one with each hand. Now *that's* dedication.

## Most Common

The most common pub name in Britain by far is **The Red Lion**. Close behind are **The Crown** and **The Royal Oak**, proving that Britain is very definitely still a monarchy. **The White Hart** and **The White Horse** complete the Top Five, with **The Black Horse** and **The White Lion** some way down the list. In a recent survey of a thousand pub names, 130 tied for bottom place with only four occurrences each in the whole kingdom. They included **California**, **The Elephant's Head**, **The Head of Steam** and **The Ferret and Trouser Leg**.

PUB FACT

There are five London tube stations named after pubs: Angel, Elephant & Castle, Manor House, Royal Oak and Swiss Cottage.

**The Top House** on the Lizard is the most southerly pub on the British mainland, and **The First and Last Inn**, in Sennan, the most westerly. But the most southerly and most westerly pub in the British Isles is **The Turk's Head** on St Agnes, one of the Isles of Scilly. The most easterly pub is **The Fisherman's Wharf** at Lowestoft's South Pier. **The Ferry Inn** at Scrabster, jumping-off point for the ship to Orkney, is the most northerly pub on mainland Britain. Although not strictly a pub, **The Baltasound Hotel**'s public bar on Unst (the most northerly island in Shetland) is where you can buy Britain's most northerly pint.

## Longest Bar

The longest bar in a British pub (and the longest in Europe too) is in Glasgow. **The Horseshoe Bar**'s horseshoe-shaped bar would be 104 ft 3 in long if you straightened it out. Though that might cause a bit of a name change.

## What the Romans Did for Us

Underfloor heating, viaducts, aqueducts, Hadrian's Wall, toga parties – the Romans introduced us to many new things. They also brought in the earliest public roadside taverns or *tabernae* to Britain. Ever since the Bronze Age we had been a nation of stay-at-home ale drinkers, but the Romans opened that particular barrel of fun and we haven't looked back since.

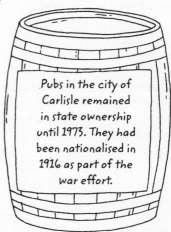

Pubs in the city of Carlisle remained in state ownership until 1973. They had been nationalised in 1916 as part of the war effort.

# Pubs in Films

Down the years there's hardly been a British film made that doesn't have one scene or other set in the pub – apart from *Watership Down*. For some actors it's their natural setting – any film with Bob Hoskins or Jason Statham must involve the pub at some point. And while some films are remembered for their sex scenes, or their chase sequences, we have chosen some great pub films, from the cult classic *Withnail and I* to the greatest lock-in of all time, *Shaun of the Dead*.

## Withnail and I (1987)

The alcoholic anarchy of cult classic *Withnail and I* required many of its scenes to be set in pubs. The Mother Black Cap in Camden Town was the real-life **Tavistock Arms** in Westbourne Green, which for a while took on its film name, which later became **The Frog and Firkin** and later still was demolished. The Crow and Crown, supposedly in Cumbria, was actually built for the film within Stockers Farm at Rickmansworth. Other rooms there served as the interior of Uncle Monty's cottage.

## An American Werewolf in London (1981)

The Slaughtered Lamb, the Yorkshire pub and starting point for the comedy horror of *An American Werewolf in London*, is actually in Surrey. And Wales. A cottage in Builth Wells stood in as its exterior. Interiors, where bit-parts were played by Rik Mayall, Brian Glover, David Schofield and others, were filmed in **The Black Swan** at Martyr's Green, Ockham (which also turns up in an episode of *Inspector Morse*).

## Passport to Pimlico (1949)

One of the best Ealing comedies, *Passport to Pimlico* looks at what it is to be British when an area of London discovers that it is in fact a part of French Burgundy. Declaring independence (and freedom from post-war rationing) Pimlico repels intervention from English bureaucrats, declaring "We'll fight them on the tramlines, we'll fight them in the local." The local in question, no longer subject to English restrictions or opening hours, is promptly renamed The Duke of Burgundy.

## The Battle of Britain (1969)

Many war films use pub settings for moments of relaxation and romance between action sequences. In *The Battle of Britain*, Squadron Leader Christopher Plummer meets his wife, Section Officer Susannah York, between Spitfire sorties in scenes filmed at **The Jackdaw Inn**, a pub near RAF Hawkinge at Denton. During the war the Jackdaw, then called The Red Lion, witnessed the real-life Battle of Britain played out in the skies overhead.

## The Long Good Friday (1980)

As you'd expect from the best ever British gangster pic, gritty pubs feature strongly in *The Long Good Friday*. It opens in Fagan's, a Belfast bar which is actually **The Salisbury** in Haringey (a location also used by Richard Attenborough in *Chaplin* and David Cronenberg in *Spider*). The Governor General pub, setting for the immortal line "Walk to the car, Billy, or I'll blow your spine off," is the real-life **Watermans Arms** on the Isle of Dogs. And rather than waste a good pub, The Lion and Unicorn (which is blown up during the action) was specially constructed on waste ground in Wapping, to the confusion of thirsty passers-by.

"In Wales it's brilliant. I go to the pub and see everybody who I went to school with. And everybody goes 'So what you doing now?' And I go, 'Oh, I'm doing a film with Antonio Banderas and Anthony Hopkins.' And they go, 'Ooh, good.' And that's it."

*Catherine Zeta-Jones*

## Get Carter (1971)

*Get Carter* was remarkable in that it was a convincing British gangster movie and that it showed a life in the north of the country as grim as southerners believed it to be. Michael Caine demonstrated his southern character's sophistication up north by asking for a pint of beer "in a thin glass" – at what used to be Europe's longest bar, in Newcastle-upon-Tyne's **North Eastern** pub. After filming one day, Caine asked for a lager and was told the bar didn't sell it "because we don't get any lasses in here." The North Eastern is long gone now, modernised and renamed, but nearby the pub seen in the film as The Vick and Comet still stands, where a young Alun Armstrong played the barman. It's now part of the O'Neills Irish theme bar chain. **The Strawberry** pub in the city, which also appears in Get Carter, is so called from being the site on which in former times nuns made strawberry wine.

## Still Crazy (1998)

Billy Connolly, Bill Nighy, Stephen Rea, Jimmy Nail and Timothy Spall play the aged former members of a rock band, Strange Fruit, contemplating a reunion gig 20 years after their last performance. There's a nod to the Stonehenge scenery debacle of another great celluloid rock band, Spinal Tap. In *Still Crazy*, the band meets up to discuss the possibility in **The Red Lion** at Avebury, unique among British pubs in sitting at the centre of a prehistoric stone circle. Old rockers amidst even older rock.

## Carry On films

Icons of bawdy British humour, the *Carry On* films have inevitably included a number of set-piece pub scenes over the years. Never likely to pass up the chance of a saucy double entendre, their pubs have included The Old Cock Inn in *Carry On Dick* (1974), and The Whippet Inn from *Carry On at Your Convenience* (1971). In *Carry on Abroad* (1972), Sid James plays a leering landlord – cue jokes about large ones and bottoms up.

### 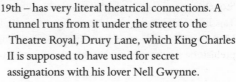 Brannigan (1975)

John Wayne (still smarting from having turned down the role of Dirty Harry) plays a no-nonsense US cop sent to Britain to extradite a wanted man. His stiff-upper-lip British counterpart is played by Richard Attenborough, and much is made of the clash of Chicago and London police cultures, especially in the use of firearms. With an eye to the American viewing public, one of the big action sequences is a fight in a pub. It was filmed in **The Lamb**, beside London's Leadenhall Market.

### Frenzy (1972)

For *Frenzy*, his second-last film, Alfred Hitchcock – son of a Covent Garden fruitmarket trader – returned to the locations of his youth to make a movie about a London serial killer. The central character, wrongly accused of the murders, works in one pub – **The Globe** on Bow Street – and drinks (heavily) in another – **Nell of Old Drury** in Covent Garden itself. A pre-Wombles Bernard Cribbins plays the unpleasant landlord of the Globe,

 which these days operates as a French bistro. The Nell – called The Lamb when it was built in the 17th century and renamed The Sir John Falstaff in the 19th – has very literal theatrical connections. A tunnel runs from it under the street to the Theatre Royal, Drury Lane, which King Charles II is supposed to have used for secret assignations with his lover Nell Gwynne.

**The Wicker Man** (1973)

Some think it's a stand-out British horror film, others think it's more like *Carry on up the Wicker Man*. This hammed up, Hammer-esque tale was filmed in Ayrshire and Galloway. Set in the spring, it was actually filmed in October and props men had to glue green leaves onto bare autumnal branches. The Green Man pub on Summerisle – in which local barmaid Britt Ekland (dazzling Swedish barmaids in the Western Isles are just *so* stereotyped, like Aussie bar staff in London) attempts to seduce Edward Woodard – is at the heart of the action. The Green Man was really two pubs; the exteriors were shot around Gatehouse of Fleet, a small Galloway village hidden in the hills behind the sea, while the interiors were in the **Ellangowan Hotel** in nearby Creetown.

### Rita, Sue and Bob Too (1987)

"Thatcher's Britain with her knickers down," proclaimed the poster for *Rita, Sue and Bob Too*. The film, about the sex lives of ordinary people, used real locations in South Yorkshire. Residents of the postwar Buttershaw estate in Bradford (in which the film's writer Andrea Dunbar also lived) were unhappy about its use in a film portraying lax moral standards. The school attended by Rita and Sue is Buttershaw High, now demolished; and the pub next to it, in which the group Black Lace perform jaunty number *Gang Bang* in the film, is **The Beacon**, and still the only pub on the estate.

> "I remember the feeling when I was doing those comedy shows in little pubs in London. I remember feeling like a real man at the end of the day. It was our show, we'd written it, we'd performed it, and I felt more alive and more like a man than I have after any days filming on a mega-budget film."
>
> *Hugh Grant*

> "A horrid alcoholic explosion scatters all my good intentions like bits of limbs and clothes over the doorsteps and into the saloon bars of the tawdriest pubs."
>
> *Dylan Thomas*

## Saturday Night and Sunday Morning (1960)

One of the first of the kitchen sink dramas of the early 1960s, *Saturday Night and Sunday Morning* had yer typical late 1950s' 'angry young man' Arthur Seaton (Albert Finney) as its central character. Arthur feels trapped by his work and family in provincial Nottingham and escapes into sex and drink. The scene in which he takes part in a drinking competition was filmed in Nottingham's **The White Horse**, now an Indian restaurant. **The British Flag**, outside which Seaton is beaten up for his affair with a married woman, is actually in Battersea. It's still open for business, unlike many of the now-demolished Nottingham streets and factories seen in the film.

## The Crying Game (1992)

The complex psychological thriller *The Crying Game* uses pubs to move the plot along in several scenes. We first meet the girlfriend of dead British soldier Forest Whitaker in The Metro Bar where she works as a singer. Set builders decorated a vacant property in Coronet Street in London for the exterior shots of the Metro, but the interior was the real interior of **The London Apprentice** pub on Old Street. Later in the film, IRA members plan the assassination of a judge over a drink in **The Lowndes Arms** in Chesham Street. Despite a campaign led by a wheelchair-bound Sir Alec Guinness, the Arms closed in 1998. The Apprentice is still going strong, and really does host music one night a week.

### Up the Junction (1968)

Another slice of social realism, *Up the Junction* is the story of a rich Chelsea girl walking away from her privileged life and slumming it in Battersea. It updates the classic portrayal of a pub singalong so often seen in British movies. Instead of a piano on the corner, there is a pop band on stage leading an open mic night; but the sense of community spirit is the same. It was filmed in **The Pavilion**, a real Battersea bar, which is largely unchanged today and still a music venue. The film is also significant for being Dennis Waterman's first major screen appearance, and for including a cameo by Queenie Watts. Queenie was an actress and singer and, in her spare time, landlady of **The Ironbridge Tavern** in Poplar along with her husband Slim.

### The Titfield Thunderbolt (1953)

Like so many Ealing studio comedies, *The Titfield Thunderbolt* is a celebration of a long lost pastoral England, full of stock English characters such as the squire, the vicar, the village policeman and of course the railway enthusiast. The very name of the village, Titfield, evokes a country idyll full of birdsong, and the village pub, The Grasshopper, conjures warm summer evenings and the distant hum of insects in the meadow. In the film a wealthy businessman is persuaded to fund a threatened branch line by a suggestion that the train will in effect be a mobile pub, not subject to the usual opening restrictions – truly, a dream pub in this Ealing dreamworld.

##  Help! (1965)

*Help!*, the second Beatles film, is defiantly zany in approach, as a sequence shot at **The City Barge** pub in Chiswick demonstrates. The lovable moptops emerge from the alley at the side of the pub, pursued by the police. On the waterfront lane outside they fall in with a marching bagpipe band, which attacks them by spraying red liquid from the pipes' drones. Pursued into the pub, the Beatles (or their stunt doubles) escape by crashing out through the pub's front windows. And finally at the bar Ringo pulls a lever disguised as a pint of beer, which opens a trapdoor beneath his feet, plunging him into the pub's cellar where he comes face to face with a tiger called Rajah. Help him if you can, he's fallen dow-ow-own. (Being a riverside pub, the City Barge actually had no cellars.)

## Local Hero (1983)

In many small Scottish communities the hotel also doubles as the public bar, and so it is in Bill Forysth's comedy *Local Hero*. The Macaskill Arms in fictional Ferness is an on-screen composite of several different locations in Scotland. The exterior was filmed at Pennan on the Moray coast with a combination of real buildings with fake walls erected between them to complete the hotel frontage. **The Pennan Inn** does a roaring trade in *Local Hero* tourism today. The Macaskill interior, in which Mac and Gordon drunkenly negotiate an exchange of life and wife over an ancient whisky ("I'd make a good Gordon, Gordon"), was filmed partly in **The Ship Inn** at nearby Banff, and partly in **The Lochailort Hotel** some 160 miles away in Morar.

## Quadrophenia (1979)

Several vanished pubs are immortalised in the film version of *Quadrophenia*, The Who's teen angst rock opera. **The Wellington Arms**, in which the anti-hero Jimmy buys fake amphetamines after his mother confiscates his stash, is sadly no more. The pub, in Archway, was bulldozed to make way for the Wellington petrol station. When the mods and rockers gather to fight in Brighton, the film gives us a glimpse of **The Heart and Hand**, now closed but at the time of filming Brighton's best known gay bar. Earlier in the film Jimmy's friend Spider is attacked by rockers outside **The Bramley Arms** in Notting Hill, which must be a contender for the BAFTA for Most Filmed Pub. Besides *Quadrophenia* it has also appeared in Ealing comedy *The Lavender Hill Mob* (1951), Harold Pinter's back-to-front *Betrayal* (1983), John Boorman's Marxist parable *Leo the Last* (1970), and Alex Cox's punk biopic *Sid and Nancy* (1986). The Bramley Arms is no longer a pub, converted a while back into exclusive residential apartments above and office space below, which no self-respecting mod, rocker or punk would be seen dead in.

## Genevieve (1953)

There's a surprisingly high pub count in the vintage car family film *Genevieve*. Although we are led to believe they all stand on the road from London to Brighton, in truth they are all to be found within a few miles of Pinewood Studios. **Ye Olde Greene Manne** at Batchworth, Herts appears as the backdrop to a scene involving a newsreel crew. The morning after the night before, Kenneth More stops at **The One Pin Inn** in Hedgerley, Bucks for a hair of the dog. **The Jolly Woodman** in Burnham, Bucks is the setting for subterfuge and sabotage, and a little later there is a failed attempt at making peace during a toilet and ice-cream stop at **The De Burgh Arms** in West Drayton. The Greene Manne, which also claims bit parts in *Withnail and I* and *Raiders of the Lost Ark*, survives, as does the Jolly Woodman. The One Pin Inn does not, bulldozed in 2009, for five 'traditional' homes.

The Bramley Arms in West London is no longer a pub but the distinctive exterior and helpful clue at the top of the building alerts location-seeking cinema buffs.

## The Hitchhiker's Guide to the Galaxy (2005)

It's a nice touch that *The Hitchhiker's Guide to the Galaxy*, a film whose very title announces vast expanses of space and time, starts off in the very intimate setting of a pub. It is there, in **The Beehive Inn** at Buntingford, Herts, that Ford Prefect gives Arthur Dent the disturbing news: the pub and the planet it stands on have been scheduled for demolition to make way for an intergalactic superhighway. But DON'T PANIC, as large friendly letters on the Guide's cover reassure us. In reality, the Beehive is, happily, under no such threat.

## Defence of the Realm (1986)

*Defence of the Realm* is a cold war political thriller about a cover-up after a nuclear bomber crashes in the English countryside. Gabriel Byrne plays an investigative journalist trying to unravel the truth, and the film has been praised for its realistic portrayal of pre-digital journalism. This means typewriters, and a lot of drinking. One of the central locations in the film is a genuine Fleet Street pub, **The Punch Tavern**. The pub used to be called **The Crown and Sugar Loaf** until the staff of *Punch* magazine took to meeting there in the 19th century. The satirical magazine, a British institution founded in Edinburgh in 1841, folded in 2002; but the pub, a British institution on the site since the 17th century, is still open.

## Shaun of the Dead (2004)

In zombie spoof *Shaun of the Dead*, B-movie fan Simon Pegg eulogises about the value of his local North London pub as a place of familiarity, comfort and safety. That's before the climax of the film, when he and long-time collaborator Nick Frost are besieged by zombie hordes in the bar of The Winchester. The film was inspired by an episode of Pegg's TV sitcom *Spaced*, and its cast draws heavily on the new comic talent in *Spaced*, *Black Books* and other more or less surreal comedy ensemble productions such as *Green Wing* and *The League of Gentlemen*. The exterior shots of the Winchester were filmed at **The Duke of Albany** in New Cross, South London.

## Hot Fuzz (2007)

Simon Pegg's follow-up to *Shaun of the Dead* also had a pub at its heart. In *Hot Fuzz* Pegg is the city cop exiled to Sandford, a country town where Nick Frost is the bumbling local bobby. Sandford is the fictional name used by the British police when they act out training scenarios, to avoid offence to any real places. Most of the film was shot in Wells, Somerset, where **The Crown at Wells** pub was used for exteriors of the fictional Sandford bar in which a climactic shoot-out takes place. William Penn, Quaker pioneer, preached from a window of the Crown in the mid-17th century, when it was already two hundred years old. **The Royal Standard** in Beaconsfield was used for the interior of the Sandford; and the church in the nearby model village of Beaconscot has the spire which proves to be the undoing of Timothy Dalton's roguish character.

## The World's End (2013)

Having sent up horror in *Shaun of the Dead* and police drama in *Hot Fuzz*, Simon Pegg takes on science fiction in *The World's End*, the third part of his Cornetto Trilogy – so-called because a different flavour of the popular ice cream is featured in each one. As they attempt 20 years later to recreate a pub crawl from their youth, five childhood friends face a challenge greater than merely completing the crawl. (There's a clue in the film's title.) The film was shot on location in the Garden Cities of Letchworth and Welwyn in an even dozen pubs, a movie-pub fan's dream. For the record they are: **The Peartree**, Welwyn (The First Post in the film); **The Doctor's Tonic**, Welwyn (appearing as The Old Familiar); **The Cork**, Welwyn (renamed The Famous Cock); **The Parkway Tavern**, Welwyn (as The Cross Hands); **Wendy's Shop,** Letchworth (The Good Companions); **The Three Magnets**, Letchworth (The Trusty Servant); **The Colonnade**, Letchworth (The Two-Headed Dog); the Broadway Cinema, Letchworth (transformed into The Mermaid); the Thai Garden restaurant, Letchworth (converted into onscreen pub The Beehive); **The Arena Tavern**, Letchworth (as the more traditionally named King's Head); Letchworth railway station (becoming The Hole in the Wall); and finally, **The Gardner's Arm**s, Letchworth (the final pub in the film crawl, The World's End). Dare you take the World's End Challenge?

# Pubs in Literature

Many of our great writers have been inspired by the pub; William Shakespeare, George Orwell, Dylan Thomas and the diarist Samuel Pepys were all in and out of the pub on a daily basis. As was *The Spectator* columnist Jeffrey Bernard who propped up the bar of the Coach and Horses in Soho for many years. He was the inspiration for the play *Jeffrey Bernard is Unwell*, the title derived from the explanation *The Spectator* ran whenever his piece failed to turn up because he was too p***ed to write it. Which was often.

# LITERATI PUBS

### The Eagle and Child, Oxford

One of the many pubs owned by the Oxford colleges, it was endowed to University College from the 17th century and part of their property portfolio until 2003 when they sold it to St John's College, which also owns **The Lamb and Flag** pub opposite. In the mid-1930s, The Eagle and Child started to host The Inklings, an Oxford writers' group which included C.S. Lewis and J.R.R. Tolkien. They would meet in a private lounge at the back of the pub known as the 'Rabbit Room', discussing their work including *The Lion, the Witch and the Wardrobe* and *The Hobbit*. Tolkien stopped attending in the late 1950s but Lewis continued until his death in 1963. Although when the pub was modernised in 1962 the Rabbit Room was altered and the group swapped pubs to the Lamb and Flag across the road.

### The Mermaid Inn, Rye

One of the oldest inns in the country and one with more history than GCSE History. This Sussex pub was burnt down by the perfidious French in a raid and a new structure rebuilt over the old cellars in the 1420s. By the early 18th century it had become the hangout of the Revenue-Men-Intolerant Hawkhurst Gang. There is a tunnel that links the cellars with **The Old Bell Inn** nearby (useful for a quick getaway). Russell Thorndike used it as a location in his Dr Syn novels – the good doctor is the Vicar of Dymchurch by day, but by night he is the smuggling, duelling 'Scarecrow'. By 1913 the Mermaid was run as a club by the mother of poet Richard Aldington. Rupert Brooke was among the many visitors, as well as American author Henry James, who lived just yards up the road at Lamb House until his death in 1916. E. F. Benson who wrote the Mapp and Lucia novels (and was also a tenant of Lamb House) was fond of giving large dinner parties at the Mermaid for his London set.

**Ye Olde Cheshire Cheese, London**

A portrait of the great dictionary compiler Samuel Johnson presides over the Cheshire Cheese, a place where he felt very much at home. He is not the only great writer to walk through its doors in a narrow alleyway off Fleet Street, it has enjoyed the custom of literary figures such as Oliver Goldsmith, Voltaire, Thackeray, Dickens, Mark Twain, Conan Doyle and G.K. Chesterton. The great Irish poet W.B. Yeats was part of the Rhymers Club of poets who met here and it included John Davidson who wrote:

> I know a house of antique ease
> Within the smoky city's pale
> A spot wherein the spirit sees
> Old London through a thinner veil.
> The modern world so stiff and stale
> You leave behind you when you please
> For long clay pipes and great old ale
> And beefsteaks in 'The Cheshire Cheese'

How he got to be a member is anyone's guess.

It was originally the boarding house of a Carmelite monastery and later the **Horn Tavern** which was destroyed by the Great Fire of 1666. The Cheshire Cheese was erected in its place the following year. Dickens employed the antique pub in *A Tale of Two Cities*. Following Charles Darnay's acquittal on charges of treason, Sydney Carton takes him off to dinner:

> Drawing his arm through his own, he took him down Ludgate Hill to Fleet Street, and so, up a covered way into a tavern. Here, they were shown into a little room, where Charles Darnay was soon recruiting his strength with a good plain dinner and good wine; while Carlton sat opposite to him at the same table, with his separate bottle of port before him.

# THREE MEN IN A PUB

Jerome K. Jerome's *Three Men in a Boat* is an account of the author's trip with two companions from Kingston upon Thames to Oxford in a large rowing skiff equipped for camping. Along the way they stopped off in many waterside taverns and pretty much gave up the idea of camping in the boat to find accommodation in inns along the route. All six pubs mentioned below (plus **The Stag** in Datchet where they failed to get a room) are still going strong.

### The George and Dragon, Wargrave

*We caught a breeze, after lunch, which took us gently up past Wargrave and Shiplake. Mellowed in the drowsy sunlight of a summer's afternoon, Wargrave, nestling where the river bends, makes a sweet old picture as you pass it, and one that lingers long upon the retina of memory. The George and Dragon at Wargrave boasts a sign, painted on the one side by Leslie, R.A., and on the other by Hodgson of that ilk. Leslie has depicted the fight; Hodgson has imagined the scene, "After the Fight", George, the work done, enjoying his pint of beer.*

### The Bull, Sonning

*If you stop at Sonning, put up at The Bull, behind the church. It is a veritable picture of an old country inn, with green, square courtyard in front, where, on seats beneath the trees, the old men group of an evening to drink their ale and gossip over village politics; with low, quaint rooms and latticed windows, and awkward stairs and winding passages.*

*We roamed about sweet Sonning for an hour or so, and then, it being too late to push on past Reading, we decided to go back to one of the Shiplake islands, and put up there for the night.*

**The Swan Inn, Pangbourne**

*The neighbourhood of Pangbourne, where the quaint little Swan Inn stands, must be as familiar to the habitués of the Art Exhibitions as it is to its own inhabitants. My friends' launch cast us loose just below the grotto, and then Harris wanted to make out that it was my turn to pull.*

 **The Beetle and Wedge, Moulsford**

This is the pub where four different locals tell the trio that it was they who caught the magnificent 18 lb trout mounted on the wall of the snug bar. Then George goes to take a closer look, knocks it off the wall and discovers it's made of plaster of Paris. The pub plays an even greater role in H.G. Wells' *The History of Mr Polly*.

 **The Barley Mow, Clifton**

*If you stay the night on land at Clifton, you cannot do better than put up at the Barley Mow. It is, without exception, I should say, the quaintest, most old-world inn up the river. It stands on the right of the bridge, quite away from the village. Its low-pitched gables and thatched roof and latticed windows give it quite a story-book appearance, while inside it is even still more once-upon-a-timeyfied.*

*It would not be a good place for the heroine of a modern novel to stay at. The heroine of a modern novel is always 'divinely tall' and she is ever 'drawing herself up to her full height'. At the Barley Mow she would bump her head against the ceiling each time she did this.*

 **The Bull, Streatley**

*We had intended to push on to Wallingford that day but the sweet smiling face of the river here lured us to linger for a while and so we left our boat at the bridge and went up in to Streatley and lunched at The Bull, much to Montmorency's satisfaction.*

**George Orwell's Perfect Pub**

'The Moon Under Water' is a 1946 essay by George Orwell, originally published in the *Evening Standard*, in which he provided a detailed description of his ideal public house, the fictitious Moon Under Water. Orwell stipulated 10 key points that his perfect London pub should have (his criteria for country pubs being different, but unspecified):

Upstairs, patrons can get a substantial lunch: for example, a cut off the joint, two vegetables and boiled jam roll— for about three bob.

The pub should be quiet enough to talk, with the establishment frowning on the use of a radio or a piano.

The barmaids know all the customers by name.

A snack counter would serve liver-sausage sandwiches, mussels, cheese, pickles and large biscuits with caraway seeds.

The architecture and fittings must be Victorian. (It's not known whether appreciating early Edwardian pubs would have counted as a 'thought crime!')

Darts and the like should only be played in the public bar.

The pub should sell a variety of handy items; tobacco and cigarettes, aspirins and stamps, and customers should be allowed to use the phone.

Apart from glass and pewter jugs, the pub should have some pleasant strawberry-pink china ones.

The pub should have a creamy sort of stout on draught, ideally served in a pewter pot. The staff are very particular about their drinking vessels at "The Moon Under Water" and never, make the mistake of serving a pint of beer in a handleless glass. That would be 'double plus bad!'

A fairly large garden should be accessible to the rear.

## The Bear, Oxford

*DEATH IS NOW MY NEIGHBOUR* **BY COLIN DEXTER**

Creator of Inspector Morse and real ale fan, Colin Dexter, was always
sending his creation off to the pub. The favourites in Oxford city centre
were **The Eagle and Child**, **The White Horse**, **The King's Arms** and
**The Bear**. But as the author explained, "Dear old John Thaw never liked
beer at all – he wasn't a great drinker". The Bear is featured in Colin
Dexter's novel *Death is Now My Neighbour*, where Morse seeks the aid of the
pub's landlords (and tie experts), Steve and Sonya Lowbridge in identifying
a tie from a photograph. That's because the distinctive feature of the Bear
is a collection of 5,000 snippets of club ties, started in 1952 by the landlord,
Alan Cours. Patrons could swap a snipped tie end for half a pint of beer
provided it wasn't in the collection. These were then pinned to the walls
and ceilings and now reside in glass cases.

## The Tabard Inn, Southwark

*CANTERBURY TALES* **BY GEOFFREY CHAUCER**

**The Tabard Inn**, from which Chaucer's 29 pilgrims set off to visit the
shrine of Thomas Becket in Canterbury – each telling a tale along the way –
was a real pub in Southwark. Its full name was The Tabard of the
Monastery of Hyde and started life as the abbot's London gaff. After the
monasteries were dissolved it became the plain old Tabard, but it was
destroyed by fire in 1669. It was rebuilt as **The Talbot** a coaching inn that
was ultimately made redundant by the railways and demolished in 1873.
The Talbot Yard still exists and a blue plaque (unveiled by *Monty Python*
medievalist Terry Jones) to the Tabard has been placed there facing rival
pub **The George** (see following entry), itself one of the oldest pubs in
London and mentioned in *The Survey of London* (1598).

## The George Inn, Southwark

*LITTLE DORRIT* **BY CHARLES DICKENS**

As can be seen from his Chigwell letter (see page 114), Dickens was a great fan of old coaching inns and a visitor to The George. In *Pickwick Papers* he wrote: "In the Borough there still remain some half dozen old inns Great rambling, queer old places with galleries, and passages, and staircases, wide enough and antiquated enough, to furnish materials for a hundred ghost stories."

The rambling old inns included the Tabard (see previous entry) and the White Hart mentioned by Shakespeare in *Henry VI* and where Mr. Pickwick first meets Sam Weller. Dickens' father was imprisoned in the Marshalsea Debtors' Prison, the setting for *Little Dorrit*, which is only a few hundred yards from the George. In Chapter 22 Amy's friend goes to deliver a begging letter from the imprisoned Mr. Dorrit to Arthur Clennam and is diverted into The George by Amy's brother so he can add his own plea.

## The Three Cripples, London

*OLIVER TWIST* **BY CHARLES DICKENS**

> The Three Cripples or rather the Cripples, which was the sign by which the establishment was familiarly known to its patrons, was the same public house in which Mr Sikes and his dog have already figured.
> Merely making a sign to a man at the bar, Fagin walked straight upstairs and opening the door of a room and softly insinuating himself into the chamber looked anxiously about, shading his eyes with his hand as if in search of some particular person.

In 1899, when the photo above was taken,
over the road from the Memorial Theatre
in Stratford-upon-Avon, the inn was known
as The Black Swan. Today it has adopted
its long-time nickname 'The Dirty Duck'
and is known as the actors' pub. Darling.

## Boar's Head Tavern, London

*HENRY V, PARTS ONE AND TWO* **BY WILLIAM SHAKESPEARE**

**The Boar's Head** tavern was a real inn located in Eastcheap near the Thames. It was the local tavern frequented by Falstaff and his gang of rowdy fellows. It was trading in 1537 but was consumed by the Great Fire of London in 1666. Shakespeare gave it a landlady, Mistress Quickly, who makes her own house rules: "I will bar no honest man in my house, nor no cheater; but I do not love swaggering."

## The Potwell Inn, Berkshire

*THE HISTORY OF MR POLLY* **BY H.G. WELLS**

The Potwell Inn is where Mr Polly finally finds his vocation. It is based on the **Beetle and Wedge** at Moulsford, the same pub described by Jerome K. Jerome in *Three Men in a Boat*. In Jerome's book it's the place where a succession of locals each describe catching the magnificent trout on the wall. In *The History of Mr Polly*, Polly takes a job at the inn as a handyman and ferryman and becomes a hero by accidentally disposing of the villain of the piece, Jim, by getting chased over a weir by him. In the course of his pursuit Jim falls and drowns in the river.

> "In many societies there is a place that constitutes a sort of neutral ground where people can meet in a public place without the strains that come from being on someone else's home ground. In West Africa, this is the space under the village's Meeting Tree. In England it is the pub. Its full title of public house is significant. Although such places seem immediately natural and non-problematic to those of the English culture, an enormous amount of cultural information has to be known in order to behave properly in such a setting."
>
> *Native Land* by Nigel Barley (1989)

## The Six Jolly Fellowship Porters, Limehouse

*Our Mutual Friend* **by Charles Dickens**

> *The Six Jolly Fellowship Porters already mentioned as a tavern of a*
> *dropsical appearance had long settled down into a state of hale infirmity.*
> *Miss Potterson sole proprietor and manager of the Fellowship Porters*
> *reigned supreme on her throne the Bar and a man must have drunk himself*
> *mad drunk indeed if he thought he could contest a point with her. "Now*
> *you mind you Riderhood," said Miss Abbey Potterson with emphatic*
> *forefinger over the half door, "the Fellowships don't want you at all and*
> *would rather by far have your room than your company."*

The pub was based on **The Grapes**, a tavern not far from Dickens'
godfather Christopher Huffan who lived in Church Row (now Nevil Street)
who was a mast, oar and block maker by trade. The Grapes was built in
1720 and is now a listed building, little changed since Dickens' day.

> *The bar of the Six Jolly Fellowship Porters was a bar to soften the human*
> *breast. The available space in it was not much larger than a hackney-coach;*
> *but no one could have wished the bar bigger, that space was so girt in by*
> *corpulent little casks, and by cordial-bottles*
> *radiant with fictitious grapes in bunches, and*
> *by lemons in nets, and by biscuits in baskets,*
> *and by the polite beer-pulls that made low*
> *bows when customers were served with beer,*
> *and by the cheese in a snug corner, and by the*
> *landlady's own small table in a snugger corner*
> *near the fire, with the cloth everlastingly laid.*

PUB
FACT

While staying at the King's Arms, on a visit to Thomas
Hardy, novelist Robert Louis Stevenson visited the
county museum in Dorchester. Looking through a
century-old book, he found the names of two local
dignitaries, Dr Jekyll and Mr Hyde. He then returned
to nearby Westbourne to write his famous novel.

**Admiral Benbow, Blackhill Cove**

*TREASURE ISLAND* **BY ROBERT LOUIS STEVENSON**

The narrator of *Treasure Island*, Jim Hawkins, is the son of the landlord of the Admiral Benbow, at Blackhill Cove on the Bristol road.

> *I take up my pen in the year of grace 17___ and go back to the time when my father kept the Admiral Benbow Inn and the brown old seaman with the sabre cut first took up his lodging under our roof. I remember him as if it were yesterday as he came plodding to the inn door his sea chest following behind him in a hand barrow a tall, strong, heavy, nut brown man, his tarry pigtail falling over the shoulders of his soiled blue coat, his hands ragged and scarred.*

"This is a handy cove and pleasant sittyated grog shop," says the old sea dog before taking up residence whilst living in constant fear of a seafaring man with a wooden leg. When he is eventually confronted, not by Long John Silver, but by Black Dog, a cutlass fight ensues. "Just at the door the captain aimed at the fugitive one last tremendous cut which would certainly have split him to the chine had it not been intercepted by our big signboard of Admiral Benbow. You may see the notch on the lower side of the frame to this day."

**Buck's Head Inn, Wessex**

*FAR FROM THE MADDING CROWD* **BY THOMAS HARDY**

Farm labourer Joseph Poorgrass is given the task of taking Fanny Robin's coffin by wagon for burial, but en route to the funeral is lured into the Buck's Head Inn. One drink leads to another – as his companions tell him: "What's yer hurry Joseph. The pore woman's dead and you can't bring her to life and you may as well sit down comfortable and finish another with us." Joseph who admits to "being a little bit drinky" already this month then gets a case of the "multiplying eye".

*"It always comes on when I have been in a public house a little time," said Joseph Poorgrass meekly. Yes I see two of every sort as if I were some holy man living in the times of King Noah and entering into the ark."*

## Jamaica Inn, Bodmin Moor

*JAMAICA INN* BY DAPHNE DU MAURIER

Jamaica Inn, built in 1750, was long the haunt of smugglers bringing in contraband from the continent along the deserted Cornish shores. Standing on the edge of Bodmin Moor in the parish of Altarnun, it was a desolate place, perfect for avoiding the revenue men. The inn had been established to provide a change of horses on the Bodmin to Launceston road across the moor (now the A30) and it was while horse riding out on the moor in 1930 that du Maurier sought refuge there after getting lost in thick fog. In the Brontë-esque novel, Mary Yellen is the young spirited woman of 23 who pitches up there to work for her aunt, despite the coachman advising her, "That's no place for a girl." She is thrust into the sub-piracy world of smugglers and wreckers co-ordinated by the burly landlord Joss Merlyn and orchestrated by the fearsome albino figure of the Vicar of Altarnun.

Jamaica Inn is unique in pub fiction, in that it is a major novel which carries the name of the pub itself. Today you can go along and enjoy the smuggling museum next door or stay in what is regarded as one of the most haunted inns in the country.

 21 Sussex Pubs

*THE FOUR MEN* BY HILAIRE BELLOC

The Pub Landlord wouldn't like it, but the half-French writer Joseph-Pierre Hilaire Belloc was a great champion of Sussex pubs and Sussex ale. His book, *The Four Men*, is almost like a Chaucerian tale – not so much *Three Men in a Boat*, as four men on a six-day pub crawl across a hundred miles of Sussex countryside, taking in 21 pubs as they go. Its four characters are The Sailor, The Poet, Grizzlebeard and 'Myself'. They set off from Robertsbridge in the east of the county to South Harting, towards the Hampshire border. The four characters represent Belloc's own personality as it changed through his life and so beneath the friendly banter there is a deeper tale to be told.

(See Pub Crawls chapter.)

## 🍺 Pubs in Cranborne, Evershot and Marnhull

*TESS OF THE D'URBERVILLES* **BY THOMAS HARDY**

There are quite a few inns and taverns dotted through Hardy's tragedy – the real-life pubs he used were:

**Fleur de Lys, Cranborne**: On Saturdays, Tess's friends would walk to the 'Flower-de-Luce' inn at nearby Chaseborough (real-life Cranborne) for a spot of merry-making. But one Saturday night Tess arrives late and is told the party has moved on to the home of a hay-trusser where she meets Alec d'Urberville and the tragedy begins to unfold.

**Acorn Inn, Evershot**: Tess passes through the village of Evershead (real-life Evershot) in West Dorset on her way to see Angel Clare's parents. "...the small town or village of Evershead, being now about half-way over the distance. She made a halt here, and breakfasted a second time, heartily enough – not at the Sow and Acorn, for she avoided inns, but at a cottage by the church." The pub also features in Hardy's tale, *The First Countess of Wessex*.

**The Crown and The Blackmore Vale, Marnhull:** Tess's home village is Marlott (real-life Marnhull), a typical Dorset village of stone and thatched cottages with two pubs Rollivers (based on the Blackmore Vale) and The Pure Drop Inn (The Crown). Tess's father tells the parson that there's a "pretty brew" in the tap at The Pure Drop, but it doesn't exceed the ale at Rollivers, which is more like a local drinking club for local people. It is at Rollivers that Tess's father first discovers they have a distant connection with the d'Urbervilles that could be to their advantage.

##  King's Arms, Dorchester

*THE MAYOR OF CASTERBRIDGE* **BY THOMAS HARDY**

For Mayor of Casterbridge read Mayor of Dorchester; like so many locations in Dorset, Thomas Hardy renamed the towns and villages of the county but used their exact streets, squares and buildings. *The Mayor of Casterbridge* revolves around the secret shame felt by Mayor Henchard after once selling his wife in a drunken stupor at the Weydon-Priors country fair before his rise to prominence. Susan Henchard eventually returns to see her now-prosperous husband holding court through the bow-fronted windows of the King's Arms. Later in the novel, with Henchard's secret revealed, his bankruptcy hearing takes place there. Hardy lived nearby and dined at the King's Arms. The inn is also mentioned in *The Trumpet Major* - and in *Far From the Madding Crowd* (where the ill-fated Farmer Boldwood carries Bathsheba inside the King's Arms to recover after she faints at the news that her 'gallant' husband, Sergeant Troy, has been drowned at sea).


## The Old Ship, Upwey

*UNDER THE GREENWOOD TREE* **BY THOMAS HARDY**

Barely changed since Hardy's time (although the mast and cross trees signboard is gone) The Ship was on the road from Casterbridge (Dorchester) to Budmouth (Weymouth). It's here that the shy and retiring carrier Dick Dewy finally plights his troth to the flighty young schoolmistress Fancy Day. Fancy is ushered into 'a little tea room' at the inn for the proposal:

*Half an hour afterwards Dick emerged from the inn, and if Fancy's lips had been real cherries probably Dick's would have appeared deeply stained. When the newly betrothed young man returned to the inn yard, the jovial publican smited him playfully under the fifth rib, and said in broad Dorset: 'This will never do, upon my life, Master Dewy! calling for tay and for a feymel passenger, and then going in and sitting down and having some too, and biding such a fine long time!'*

## The Newman Arms, London

*1984* BY GEORGE ORWELL

George Orwell knew this Rathbone Street pub well. He used it as the model for the prole, underclass pub **The George** in his classic *1984*, and it looked the part. An unofficial blue plaque celebrates the memory of the former landlord: "Joe Jenkins, ex-proprietor, poet, bon viveur and Old Git, regularly swore at everybody on these premises," it reads.

## Chequers, Fowlmere, Cambs

*THE DIARY OF SAMUEL PEPYS*

Although he was the son of a tailor in Fleet Street, Samuel Pepys family came from Cambridgeshire and he would often travel back to his uncle Robert's farm in Brampton on horseback. Thus he frequently required the accommodation of an inn and stabling en route. On 24th February 1660 he dined and lodged at the Chequers in Fowlmere – as his diary entry attests:

> *I rose very early, and taking horse at Scotland Yard, at Mr. Garthway's stable, I rode to Mr. Pierce's, who rose, and in a quarter of an hour, leaving his wife in bed (with whom Mr. Lucy methought was very free as she lay in bed), we both mounted, and so set forth about seven of the clock, the day and the way very foul. About Ware we overtook Mr. Blayton, brother-in-law to Dick Vines, who went thenceforwards with us, and at Puckeridge we baited, where we had a loin of mutton fried, and were very merry, but the way exceeding bad from Ware thither. Then up again and as far as Foulmer, within six miles of Cambridge, my mare being almost tired: here we lay at the Chequer, playing at cards till supper, which was a breast of veal roasted.*

The Chequers is still in business today and the diary entry is framed and posted near the door. During World War II the pub became the favoured drinking haunt of the RAF's No 19 Squadron and then the American 339th fighter Group

Pepys went on from the Chequers to **The Falcon Inn** at 9 Petty Cury, Cambridge (demolished to create the Lion Yard shopping centre) and the following day saw him supping in **The Three Tuns** on Market Hill by St Edwards Passage (closed in 1790): "to the Three Tuns where we drank pretty hard and many healths to the King & co till it began to be darkish, then we broke up and I and Mr Zanchy went to Magdalene College where a very handsome supper at Mr Hill's chambers."

Pepys was also a fan of the Black Bull in Brampton which rejoiced in a landlady by the name of Goody Stankers who brewed her own beer, "fresh with a taste of worme wood which ever after did please me very well".

### The King's Head, Chigwell

#### DICKENS' PUBLISHED LETTERS

"Chigwell, my dear fellow, is the greatest place in the world. Name your day for going. Such a delicious old inn opposite the churchyard – such a lovely ride – such beautiful scenery – such an out-of-the-way rural place!"

The 'delicious old inn' was the King's Head which served as the Mapypole Inn of *Barnaby Rudge*. Dickens described it as:

*…more gable ends than a lazy man would care to count on a sunny day; huge zig-zag chimneys out of which it seemed as though even smoke could not choose but to come in more than naturally fantastic shapes imparted to it in its tortuous progress…Its windows were diamond pane lattices…Its floors were sunken and uneven, its ceilings blackened by the hand of time and heavy with massive beams.*

## CELEBRITY PUB

**Ye Olde King's Head** in
Chigwell really is olde. It was
built in 1547 and its exterior has
black and white half-timbered
beams. Since 2009 it has been
owned by local resident **Lord
Alan Sugar**, who has installed
Sheesh, his favourite Turkish
restaurant, within the pub's
former ballroom.

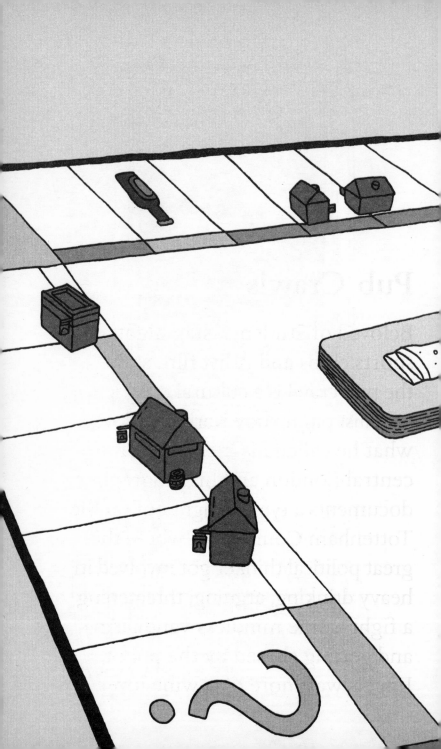

# Pub Crawls

Beloved of students, stag nights, sports clubs and A-list film stars, the pub crawl is a cultural experience. Socialist pin-up boy Karl Marx loved what he called his 'beer trips' in central London and his biographer documents a typical night out on the Tottenham Court Road where the great political thinker got involved in heavy drinking, arguing, threatening a fight, some mindless vandalism and getting chased by the police. Engels was more of a wine lover.

##  The Oliver Reed Pub Crawl

The patron saint of the pub, Oliver Reed, was well known in the pubs of Wimbledon. In what looks like an early version of pub golf, he would make two circuits of eight pubs. The aim was to drink a pint in less than fifteen minutes and then move on to the next alehouse – thus eight could be managed in around two hours. It is said that one time Steve McQueen flew in to discuss a movie project with Reed and his reward for tagging along with Ollie was to have the big man throw up on him. The pubs:

**The Hand in Hand**
**The Crooked Billet**
**The Fox and Grapes**
**Rose and Crown**
**Firestables**
**The Brewery Tap**
**The Dog and Fox**
**Finch's** (now closed)

A favourite pub crawl is 'The 12 Pubs of Christmas'. It's impossible to find pubs called the Four Calling Birds, they can be any pubs, but participants must wear a Christmas jumper.

## The Inter-Counties Pub Crawl

How many different English counties can you drink in during the course of an evening? The answer is at least 11. The author has a particular interest in this pub crawl as he was at the wheel of the car that conveyed three fellow drinking students around the shires of England in 1979 to establish the first Inter-Counties Pub Crawl Record. Here's the list:

Gloucestershire, **The King Dick**, Bristol (5.30)
Somerset, **The Curfew**, Bath (6.10)
Wiltshire, **The Borough Arms**, Swindon (6.57)
Berkshire, **The Prince of Wales**, Kingston Bagpuize (7.26)
Oxfordshire, **The Coach and Horses**, Clifton Hampden (8.02)
Buckinghamshire, **The County Arms**, Aylesbury (8.35)
Hertfordshire, **The Anchor**, Tring (8.52)
Bedfordshire, **The Ship**, Leighton Buzzard (9.17)
Northamptonshire, **The Plough**, Brackley (9.52)
Warwickshire, **Chequers**, Stratford-upon-Avon (10.30)
Worcestershire, **The Norton Grange**, Evesham (10.58)

We knew this record could easily be beaten because it was done in a 600cc Citroen Dyane (like a 2CV) whose acceleration was 0–60 in about 28 seconds. With four blokes sitting inside, that lengthened to about a couple of days. You'll be reassured to know that the driver took no part in the drinking and watched helplessly as the map-reading skills of his companions disintegrated around Buckinghamshire.

**Six-Day Sussex Pub Crawl**

Bob Copper was a 'folklorist' who embraced Hilaire Belloc's philosophy about the English pub and was so taken with his extended-pub-crawl-novel, *The Four Men* (see Pubs in Literature chapter), that he decided to retrace the journey. Belloc's original journey had been in 1902 and Copper repeated it for his book *Across Sussex with Belloc*, first in the 1950s and again in the 1990s. Bob visited the same pubs but also slipped in a few of his own.

Day 1: Robertsbridge to Uckfield (19 miles)
**The George** (Robertsbridge)
**Three Cups Inn** (Three Cups Corner)
**Blackboys Inn** (Blackboys)
**Ye Maiden's Head Inn** (Uckfield)
Day 2: Uckfield to Pease Pottage (20 miles)
**Rose & Crown** (Fletching)
**Sheffield Coach House** (Fletching)
**Black Swan** (Pease Pottage)
Day 3: Pease Pottage to Ashurst (17 miles)
**Crabtree Inn** (Crabtree)
**Countryman Inn** (Shipley)
**The George Inn** (Henfield),
**Fountain Inn** (Ashurst)
Day 4: Ashurst to Storrington (10 miles)
**Chequer Inn** (Steyning)
**Frankland Arms** (Washington)
**White Horse** (Storrington)
Day 5: Storrington to Duncton (12 miles)
**Sportsman Inn** (Amberley)
**Black Horse** (Amberley)
**Houghton Bridge Inn** (Amberley)
**George & Dragon** (Houghton)
Day 6: Duncton to South Harting (13 miles)
**Cricketers' Arms** (Duncton)
**Forrester's Arms** (Graffham)
**Greyhound** (Cocking Causeway)
**Three Horseshoes Inn** (Elsted)

## Mumbles Mile, Swansea

The Mumbles Mile is a stretch of pubs on the Mumbles Road in Mumbles facing out into Swansea Bay. At one time it boasted more than 20 drinking establishments, but now that number has been reduced to nine. The mile is still popular with pub crawlers, students and on Fridays and Saturdays, stag and hen parties (who dress for the occasion and especially enjoy gurning or mooning at the windows of the many restaurants now jammed in between the pubs).

## Transpennine Real Ale Trail, Yorkshire and Lancashire

Those redoubtable seekers of a fine beverage, Oz and James (Clarke and May), made this particular pub crawl famous by including it in their *Oz and James Drink to Britain* programme in 2009. It starts (or finishes) at the Victorian buffet bar at Stalybridge. This is a pub crawl by train, stopping at six stations in Yorkshire and Lancashire, each with a designated pub within staggering distance. Trains run hourly so there's time to savour a range of real ales and not get all Oliver Reed about it.

PUB FACT

Pub crawls are livened up by a series of spurious rules that include: No talking about sport, no talking about school/college, drinking with your left hand, and calling each other by an assumed name.

> "In my hometown there is a pub named after me – The Frome Flyer on Jenson Avenue. How cool is that?"
>
> *Jenson Button*

##  Monopoly Pub Crawl, London

The best-known of themed pub crawls takes in all 26 London streets and stations on the famous Monopoly board. Much like the game, it takes an eternity to complete and a lot of money changes hands, though in this game everybody ends up worse off. It can be tackled a number of ways. Attempted in board order, it begins south of the river on the Old Kent Road and ends up in the swanky environs of Mayfair. The official version of the pub crawl, with designated pubs and bars, is such a regular crowd-puller that **The George** (40 Tower Bridge Road, close to the startline, Old Kent Road) opens at 10.30am on a Saturday especially.

## Seven-Legged Bar Crawl, Nottingham

The story goes that when Sir Jesse Boot (of the Chemist empire) donated the land that would become Nottingham University campus, in 1921, he stipulated that on one day of the year students should have themselves some fun. Glossing over the fact that he needn't have worried about students working too hard, the 'tradition' has manifested itself today – via rag weeks – as a seven-legged bar crawl. Six people in themed fancy dress are tied together while a seventh unfettered member gets the drinks in. Over 6,000 people have taken part in the past, raising money for charity and having a laugh. Although the toilet breaks must be complicated.

## Pub Golf

For 200 years, Britain has led the way in inventing sports and as the home of the pub it naturally falls upon Blighty to set the rules of Pub Golf. Pub Golf can be played over either nine or 18 holes – although for 18 you may need a large town or city (or a caddie to drive you between holes).

Dress: Ideally participants should wear golf attire – nasty nylon trousers or slacks, Pringle jumpers and polo shirts, plus a golfing glove to improve the grip on the glass. Golf spikes are not necessary and can get you thrown off the course.

Rules: Before the game commences, it must be decided what the drink is for each hole and how many sips it must be downed in – i.e. par 3, par 4 or par 5.

Hazards: Hazards can be applied to holes – such as a ban on use of the pub's toilet at one hole (penalty strokes apply), or a ban on foodstuffs.

Penalties: There are penalty strokes added for failing to drink your bevvy in the required number of sips, for spilling your drink, for accidentally drinking someone else's drink, or slow play.

Scoring: Score cards are necessary, but like real golf, players must mark their fellow competitor's cards.

For those who want Pub Golf to emulate the professional game, there should be a 'cut' halfway through the competition to eliminate the bottom half. In Pub Golf this is known as the Half-Cut.

If you live near Milton Keynes you can dress up and go on the annual Stony Stratford Zombie Pub Crawl.

www.zombiepubcrawl.co.uk

## 🍾 A London Pub Crawl with Karl Marx, late 1850s

Karl Marx was the Oliver Reed of revolutionary socialism. His great friend and benefactor Engels was a bon viveur who liked his wine, but it was Marx who was always down the pub. He often frequented **The Museum Tavern** opposite the British Museum and when his friend Edgar Bauer dropped in on him he suggested what biographer Wilhelm Liebknecht described as a "beer trip" in central London. Typical of many British pub crawls, it involved lots of drinking, boasting, followed by a heated argument, flying fists, a hasty exit, some mindless vandalism and a police chase. Liebknecht writes in perfect teutonic style, so imagine Herr Flick reading this out:

*One evening, Edgar Bauer, acquainted with Marx from their time in Berlin together, and then not yet his enemy, had come into town from Highgate for the purpose of "making a beer trip".*

*The idea was to "take something" in every saloon between Oxford Street and Hampstead Road – making the something a very difficult task, even by confining yourself to a minimum, considering the enormous number of saloons in that part of the city. But we went to work undaunted and managed to reach the end of Tottenham Court Road without accident.*

*There, loud singing issued from a public house; we entered and learned that a club of Odd Fellows were celebrating a festival. We met some of the men belonging to the "party," and they at once invited us "foreigners" with truly English hospitality to go with them into one of the rooms. We followed them in the best of spirits, and the conversation naturally turned to politics – we had been easily recognised as German fugitives; and the Englishmen, good old-fashioned people, who wanted to amuse us a little, considered it their duty to revile thoroughly the German princes and the Russian nobles. By "Russian" they meant Prussian nobles. Russia and Prussia are frequently confounded in England, and not alone of account of their similarity of name. For a while, everything went smoothly. We had to drink many healths and to bring out and listen to many a toast.*

*Then the unexpected suddenly happened... Edgar Bauer, hurt by some chance remark, turned the tables and ridiculed the English snobs. Marx launched an enthusiastic eulogy on German science and music – no other country, he said, would have been capable of producing such masters of music as Beethoven, Mozart, Handel and Haydn, and the Englishmen who had no music were in reality far below the Germans who had been prevented hitherto only by the miserable political and economic conditions from accomplishing any great practical work, but who would yet outclass all other nations. So fluently I have never heard him speak English.*

*For my part, I demonstrated in drastic words that the political conditions in England were not a bit better than in Germany, the only difference being that* we Germans knew our public affairs were miserable, while the Englishmen did not know it, whence it were apparent that we surpassed the Englishmen in political intelligence.

The brows of our hosts began to cloud and when Edgar Bauer brought up still heavier guns and began to allude to the English cant, then a low "damned foreigners!" issued from the company, soon followed by louder repetitions. Threatening words were spoken, the brains began to be heated, fists were brandished in the air and we were sensible enough to choose the better part of valour and managed to effect, not wholly without difficulty, a passably dignified retreat.

Now we had enough of our "beer trip" for the time being, and in order to cool our heated blood, we started on a double quick march, until Edgar Bauer stumbled over some paving stones. "Hurrah, an idea!" And in memory of mad student pranks he picked up a stone, and Clash! Clatter! a gas lantern went flying into splinters. Nonsense is contagious – Marx and I did not stay behind, and we broke four or five street lamps – it was, perhaps, 2 o'clock in the morning and the streets were deserted in consequence. But the noise nevertheless attracted the attention of a policeman who with quick resolution gave the signal to his colleagues on the same beat. And immediately countersignals were given. The position became critical.

Happily we took in the situation at a glance; and happily we knew the locality. We raced ahead, three or four policemen some distance behind us. Marx showed an activity that I should not have attributed to him. And after the wild chase had lasted some minutes, we succeeded in turning into a side street and there running through an alley – a back yard between two streets – whence we came behind the policemen who lost the trail. Now we were safe. They did not have our description and we arrived at our homes without further adventures.

A young Joseph Stalin first met Vladimir Ilyich Lenin at the Crown and Anchor (now The Crown) on Clerkenwell Green. Lenin had recently moved the publication of the Russian socialist newspaper *Islra* to the hotbed of left-wing thought that was Clerkenwell when the starry-eyed Stalin came to London to train as a Bolshevik.

## Pub Golf in Cirencester, Gloucestershire

Following on from Pub Golf (see page 123), here's a cheeky little nine holes in Cirencester.

**Somewhere Else**, 65 Castle Street
**Mad Hatter**, 32 Castle Street
**MacKenzies**, 34 Castle Street
**The Black Horse**, 17 Castle Street
**The Crown** (Slug & Lettuce), 17 West Market Place
**The Golden Cross**, 20 Black Jack Street
**Bear Inn**, 12 Dyer Street
**The Wheatsheaf Inn**, 79 Cricklade Street
**Twelve Bells**, 12 Lewis Lane

## Piddle Valley Crawl

A pub crawl with an irresistible name devised by Bob Rosenthal – it refers to the Dorset Piddle as opposed to the Piddle Brook in Worcestershire that runs through Wyre Piddle. The official drink for this crawl is pints of beer – although French participants might fancy asking for a bottle of Pisse Vielle from the Rhone Valley (translated as Old Piddle).

**Sun Inn**, Charminster
**Inn 4 All Seasons**, Charminster
**Smiths Arms**, Godmanstone
**Royal Oak**, Cerne Abbas
**Red Lion**, Cerne Abbas
**New Inn**, Cerne Abbas

**Piddle Inn**, Piddletrenthide
**European Inn**, Piddletrenthide
**Thimble**, Piddlehinton
**Digby Tap**, Sherborne
**Half Moon**, Sherborne
**Plume of Feathers**, Sherborne

## The Julia Bradbury Pub Crawl

### (A.K.A. A PUB CRAWL ROUND AMBLESIDE)

*Country File* presenter Julia Bradbury doesn't need much of an invitation to strap on a kagoule and get her hobnailed boots out. If she's not strolling up and down canal towpaths, she's scaling the heights of the Lake District, a copy of *Wainwright's Walks* in her hand. So this pub circuit is ideal for one of those days when the cloud comes down and filming is impossible.

**The Churchill** (Winston's Bar), Lake Road, Ambleside
**Royal Oak**, Lake Road, Ambleside
**The White Lion**, Lake Road, Ambleside
**Ambleside Salutation Hotel**, Lake Road, Ambleside
**Queen's Hotel**, Market Place, Ambleside
**The Ambleside Tavern**, Compston Road, Ambleside
**The Unicorn**, North Road, Ambleside
**The Golden Rule**, Smithy Brow, Ambleside
**Wateredge Inn**, Waterhead.

Devised by the Westmorland Branch of the Campaign for Real Ale.

"The very first time I did the pub landlord was with Harry Hill, when we were doing this pub band thing. The whole idea was that the act hadn't turned up so the landlord of the bar was filling in. Initially, he was very reluctant to be on stage – he had opinions and was fond of the sound of his own voice but didn't really want to be there. But that very quickly fell away because it didn't work in a cabaret environment."

*Al Murray – The Pub Landlord*

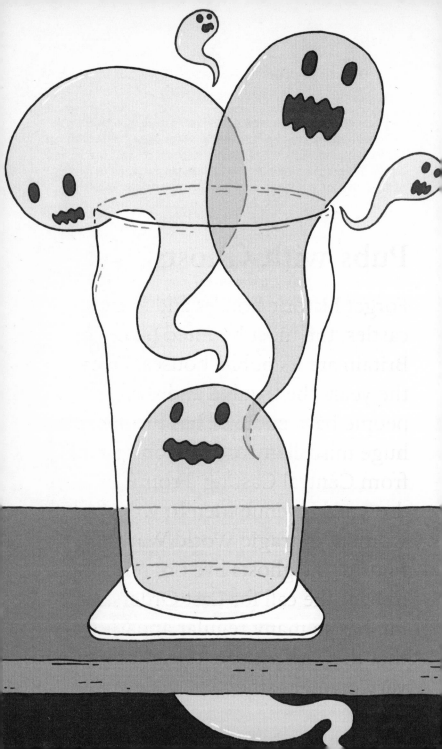

# Pubs with Ghosts

Forget historic houses and ancient castles, the most haunted places in Britain are its public houses. Over the years the trouble and strife people have endured has produced a huge miscellany of walk-on spooks from Central Casting. From drowned revenue men to wronged women, to tragic World War II figures, the ghosts live on, refusing to hear the call for Last Orders. One inn has so many regular apparitions that they ask visitors to sign their very own ghostbook...

## 🍾 Skirrid Rigid

**The Skirrid Inn** near Abergavenny has a strong claim as Britain's most haunted pub. For over five hundred years it doubled as the local courtroom, and convicted prisoners were routinely hanged from its rafters until dead. Now they're back, slamming doors, appearing at windows, levitating money and smashing glasses at a rate of 10 or so a week. You may hear soldiers and their horses in the courtyard, and catch a glimpse of the White Lady, Father Henry Vaughan or Fanny Price, three of the ghostly regulars at the Skirrid. Visitors sometimes smell Fanny's perfume and hear the rustle of her skirts as she passes, and one claimed that she had tried to drown him in the bath. In the stairwell, where the hangings took place, many guests have felt choked and dizzy; some report feeling a noose being placed over their heads, and the marks of the rope remaining on their necks for days afterwards.

## 🔫 Very Last Orders

Some ghosts are just mischievous. **The King Billy** (more formally **The King William IV**) in Kingsthorpe, Northants, has a handful of jokers from the nether world meddling in the pub's affairs. One of them, also called Bill, should know better, as he was a former landlord from the 1970s. Between them they slam doors, set off fire alarms, turn off the gas bottles in the cellar and pop the corks of the bottled ales. None of which is good for business.

## 🎯 Hells Bells and…

You can probably guess how **The New Inn** at Phillack in Cornwall, now called **The Bucket of Blood**, got its current name. Many years ago its water supply came from a well. After the publican drew the eponymous bucketful of gore instead of clear water, the well was searched and the corpse of a missing customs officer found at the bottom. Having presumably perished at the hands of smugglers, the ghostly spirit of the dead official is now regularly seen and heard by a more law-abiding modern-day clientele.

## Stones in His Pocket

Perhaps it's the name of **The Devil's Stone Inn** in Shebbear, Devon, which attracts its many ghosts. By and large they're a cheerful lot. They include a friendly seven-year-old girl, often accompanied by a grey-bearded old man; but a grumpy old rent collector is also among the regular spooks. The pub is named after a large rock in the village which is said to have fallen from the devil's pocket while he was falling from heaven to hell. For those of us who have had to reverse for a mile down a narrow Devon lane to find space for a caravan to pass, hell is not actually that far away.

## Well Dead

As befits a pub at the meeting place of two ley lines, **The Red Lion** at Avebury, Wilts, plays host to some energetic spirits. And probably a lot of men with beards and grooming issues. One paranormal investigator said he found new scratches on his neck after a night's observation in the 17th-century building. Paranormal activity or just quality control issues in Primark's value pyjamas? Florrie, a former landlady of the pub, still appears to guests despite having been murdered 350 years ago by her soldier husband for infidelity. The phantom of a young girl who was thrown down the pub's 86-foot well (notice a familiar theme arising...?) still haunts the place, and if you're lucky you will either see or hear – but never both – a spectacular but ghostly coach and horses.

## Grenadiers For Fears

**The Grenadier** pub in Belgravia, London is so called having been the officers' mess for the Grenadier Guards, the Duke of Wellington's regiment. When one September an officer was caught cheating at cards (damnable rogue) by his colleagues, they dished out some rough military justice in the form of a severe beating. The offending player was thrown down the pub stairs and died. Now his footsteps can be heard on the stairs, his face seen at windows, and his groans heard in the cellar. Ghostly activity reaches a peak each September.

 **Out For a Sinful**

The Hellfire Club was an 18th-century society for wealthy fops, their motto 'Do What Thou Wilt', at which they indulged in sinful acts of depravity and devil worship. In polite society it was referred to as the Order of the Friars of St Francis of Wycombe, after its founder Sir Francis Dashwood, and they met at **The George and Dragon** in West Wycombe, Bucks. A young servant girl at the inn who had been present at one of their meetings was found dead the following day, and as the White Lady she still walks through the pub today. No doubt trying to find the well...

## The Ancient Ram in Wootton-under-Edge

**The Ancient Ram** in Wotton-under-Edge, Gloucs had lain derelict for some years before the owner John Humphries bought the 12th-century property for a song in 1968. He soon found out why. On his first night there, cold hands pulled him from his bed. Ancient graves have been found beneath the pub, and the ghosts of a former landlord and a woman haunt the place. Customers have heard footsteps and a child crying; and when the present owner hung a portrait of the Reverend John Wesley in the stairwell, there was a surge in paranormal activity. Although there is now no family pet, the Humphries children regularly saw a mysterious black cat, that needed no flap to get in and out of the pub.

## Beware of the Tug

There aren't many tales of phantom animals, but **The Golden Fleece** in York has one – a haunting hound which tugs at the trouser legs of customers as if trying to warn them of something. Like Skippy the Bush Kangaroo but on four legs. Perhaps it's the death of another of the ghosts which drives the dog. A Canadian airman who committed suicide there in 1945 now appears in uniform by the window from which he jumped. Lady Alice Peckett, daughter of an 18th-century owner of the Fleece, regularly walks the corridors. If you sit in the wrong seat in the bar, the ghost of one of its former occupants is said to let you know 'in no uncertain terms'. Presumably it hates pack-outs on Saturday nights.

### 🎸 Signing the Ghostbook

The setting of **The Jamaica Inn**, high and isolated on Bodmin Moor, would be enough to give you the jitters on a misty night. So frequent are the sightings of ghosts here that the pub keeps a special logbook in which visitors can record their paranormal experiences. (See Pubs in Literature chapter.) Horses hooves clatter on invisible cobbles outside, while in the bar the footsteps of a long dead smuggler suggest he's returning to finish his drink. The apparition of an old sailor often occupies the same spot on a wall in front of the inn; and in an upstairs room a figure in long coat and tricorn hat crosses the floor and disappears through a wardrobe.

### 🌍 Wuthering Nights

Haworth in West Yorkshire is famous as the home of the Brontës. The three sisters and their brother all died young, their talents underexploited, and it is the restless ghost of the brother Branwell which still haunts the bar of **The Fleece Inn** in the village, where in life he was a regular customer. Although in this case 'regular customer' is a euphemism for raging alcoholic.

### Well Attractive

Eliza Jane Mackay can find her way to the bar with her eyes closed. She was an alcoholic who drank at **The Old Original** pub on High Moor between Oldham and Saddleworth. One terrible night, on her drunken way home, she drowned herself in the well of a nearby farm. To this day she still returns to the Old Original for one last drink, and her blurred phantom beats the same well-worn path through the pub each time it appears.

### Not Laughing Cavalier

If you feel someone tap you heavily on the shoulder in **The Ring O' Bells** pub in Manchester, don't feel you need to turn around: there won't be anybody there. If you hear footsteps coming down the stair, don't be surprised if no one arrives: it's only Edward, the Sad Cavalier. Edward does sometimes appear himself, in high 17th-century fashion, a mostly harmless soul mourning his own death and sliding a glass along the bar from time to time. Once, however, back in 1972, he threw a stone at the landlord who was checking the barrels in the cellar.

PUB FACT

Pluckley in Kent gets the nod in *The Guinness Book of World Records* as Britain's Most Haunted Village, and The Dering Arms is the most haunted of its three haunted pubs. In the front bar, the ghost of a kindly old lady in a bonnet is so solid that many people mistake her for a paying customer.

## Two Ghosts Walk into a Pub

They say that all ghosts are trying to tell us something. Two of them turned up in the bar of **The King's Arms** in Monkton Farleigh, Wilts during building work in the 1990s, and told the barmaid, "No good will come of this." When the builders knocked through a wall, they found a key which fitted none of the ancient pub's locks. It hangs now in the bar, waiting for no good to come of it. Elsewhere in the pub customers and staff regularly hear a sobbing woman and the sound of footsteps. The pub is built on the site of an 11th-century priory, and a mischievous monk who died there has been known to move objects around just for fun. The lane outside was the scene of a 19th-century traffic accident when a horse-drawn carriage ran out of control and crashed into the King's Arms, killing the woman driving it. Today the clatter of horses' hooves and her dying screams can still be heard.

## Oh no, it's the Mysterious Fish Lady

When the barman of **The Ship Inn** at Sandgate, Kent went to deal with an intruder whom he had spotted on a security camera, his barmaid watched him from a safe distance on CCTV. He found the corridor empty, but she saw him walk straight through the body of the stranger. It was another sighting of the Ship's Fish Lady, a Victorian woman known to discomfort customers of whom she disapproves. The building used to be a fishmonger's shop, but she is probably the wife of a former landlord who died suddenly in 1848. The verdict of the inquest into her death was 'died by the visitation of God'. 'Mysterious fish lady', sounds more like something invented by Noel Fielding in *The Mighty Boosh*.

 **The Doom Bar**

**The St Anne's Castle** pub in Great Leighs, Essex is mentioned in the
Domesday Book and served pilgrims heading for Canterbury in the 12th
century. That may explain the spirits of malevolent monks who hide objects
and switch electrical appliances on and off around the building. The Anne
in its name may be Anne Hughes, who was put to death for witchcraft in
1621. She and her black cat, who both haunt the pub now, are just two of a
huge cast of characters from the past who are still present. There's George
Benfield, hanged in 1875 for murdering his wife and son when he discovered
the son was in fact his brother's child. There's Elizabeth, who paces an
upstairs room in her wedding dress, waiting for her groom. The apparitions
of two small children, a boy and a girl, play together; and an invisible pipe
smoker scents the air in the bar when he lights up. One room upstairs is so
charged with sadness and death that the landlady keeps it locked at all times.

## Don't Enrage 'John The Jibber'

One of the most unusual pubs in Britain is **The Marsden Grotto** at South
Shields. Set in caves enlarged in 1782 with dynamite, it is unreachable at
high tide except by a precarious zig-zag path up the cliff and, from 1938,
a lift. Its inaccessibility in the early 19th century made it very attractive to
smugglers. When one of them, John the Jibber, turned informant for the
local customs officers, his colleagues handed out rough justice by
suspending him in a barrel from the ceiling of one of the caves and leaving
him to starve to death. His ghost haunts the pub, and until the 1980s used to
drain a tankard of ale left out for it every night. When a local DJ drank the
beer instead, Smuggler John was so incensed that he hurled ashtrays about
and turned on the taps overnight, flooding the cellar.

## 🍾 The Lesser of two Nevilles

Is it possible for a ghost to haunt a building which was not there when the ghost became a ghost? **The Volunteer** in London's Baker Street poses this question. The site on which it stands was occupied by the powerful Neville family in the 17th century. In 1654 a disastrous fire broke out, destroying their mansion and burning to death the unpopular Nevilles (a bunch of bullies and gangsters). Only the cellars survived, on which a hundred years later the Volunteer was erected. Now Rupert, one of the younger Nevilles, clad in coat, stockings and breeches, is said to inhabit not just his old cellars but the rest of the building too. His footsteps echo around the place and he tampers with the electrics too, something else that didn't exist in his day.

## 🗝 Spanish Stroll

Dick Turpin's father was once the landlord of **The Spaniard's Inn** in Hampstead, and there are those who claim to hear the ghostly hooves of Dick's mount Black Bess racing past. But the pub gets its name from two earlier landlords, Juan and Francesco Porero. The two Spaniards fell in love with the same woman and came to blows over her. In a duel, Francesco killed Juan, who is buried nearby and now haunts the popular pub. A shadowy woman in white, perhaps the object of their affections, is often seen in the beer garden, after a long hot Sunday afternoon's drinking. Or maybe it's smoke from the barbecue...

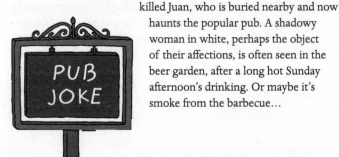

What do you call a pub that serves just rum and cigars, and where the only dish on the menu is rice-and-beans?
Answer: A Castro pub.

 **Spirit Spills Beer**

From 1843, Millbank Prison in Pimlico was used to house criminals sentenced to transport overseas before they were shipped out to the penal colonies. The pub immediately outside it, The Morpeth Arms, was built in 1845 to satisfy the thirst of their warders. It is the ghosts of inmates rather than jailers which haunt the pub today. It sits in part above underground corridors of solitary confinement cells radiating out from the prison, and in one of those cells a prisoner committed suicide rather than be sent so far from all he loved. Now his unseen hands knock drinks from the grasp of the pub clientele, and hurl bottles and glasses violently to the floor. Also, it's a great excuse for clumsy barmen.

## The Ghost That Thinks It's Oz Clarke

A 17th-century gallows once stood on the site of The Court Oak pub in Harborne, and the ghost of an innocent young woman hung for infanticide now lurks in the bar at night. Another presence has been nicknamed 'Corky' because of his habit of smashing bottle after bottle of cheap wine in the pub's cellars. The phantom wine critic, a man of about 60, has been seen behind the bar too; and Corky stops breaking bottles only when the landlord improves the selection of house wines.

The trick to getting the bar staff's attention is to stand up straight and try to make eye contact with them without being ostentatious. Follow the person who is serving your section of the bar with your eyes. If you make eye contact, merely raise your eyebrows briefly, or slightly raise your chin as if to say "yes, I have acknowledged your presence and you have acknowledged mine. I'm not making a big thing out of it, though." Do NOT under ANY circumstances be the w***er who says "Me next mate, yeah?" — as this will only make the bar staff not want to serve you and increases the likelihood that there will be spit in your beer.

*TVtropes.org on 'Getting Served at the British Pub'*

## CELEBRITY PUBS

**Piers Morgan** had a big year in 2010.
He was picked to fill the US TV chat show
slot vacated by retiring legend Larry King;
he married his second wife; and he bought
himself a little piece of England,
**The Hansom Cab** pub in Kensington.
The Victorian institution now belongs to
Piers and his brother Rupert, and the pub
grub is by Morgan's business partner in the
venture, top chef Marco Pierre White.

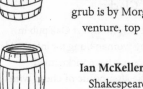

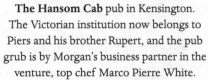

**Ian McKellen** is one of England's finest
Shakespearean actors. But it was his
earnings from work as Gandalf in the
Lord of the Rings film trilogy that gave him
the cash to become a pub owner. He
bought his local pub, **The Grapes** in
Limehouse, a pub frequented by Dickens
and portrayed as The Six Jolly Fellowship
Porters in *Our Mutual Friend*.

# Pubs in the News

Pubs are always making the news – women give birth in them, footballers are arrested in them and sometimes prime ministers leave their eight-year-old daughters there. And when it comes to a visit by a foreign dignitary, prime ministers of all shades like to emphasize the Britishness of the occasion by taking them down the pub – bar bill £28, security bill £46,500.

### 🍾 The Blood of Our Lord – The Crisps of Our Lord

Running a small pub is a big commitment. So when the Fairhursts, hosts at **The Swan Inn** in North Warnborough, Hants, entered a competition and won a luxury holiday in 2009, it seemed unlikely they would be able to get away. Step forward vicar Gary Keith of All Saints Church in nearby Odiham. Gary, clearly the answer to the Fairhursts' prayers, offered to cover for them, exchanging holy communion wine for two pints of lager and a packet of crisps. The *Daily Mirror*, in reporting the story, quoted landlady Jo Fairhurst as saying, "He's been our saviour." It sounds like the perfect plotline for an episode of 'Rev'.

### 🍾 A Ploughman's for the Cowboy

President George W. Bush wound up his November 2003 state visit to England not with a banquet but a pub lunch. His last day was spent in the company of Tony Blair, on an informal tour of the prime minister's Sedgefield constituency. Together the two men who had just taken the western world into war with Iraq had fish and chips and non-alcoholic lager in **The Dun Cow**. Hosts Geoff and Mishy Rayner had previously entertained Blair and his French counterpart Lionel Jospin, although they admitted that "there was a different standard of security" for Bush's visit.

PUB FACT

The lowest pub in England is The Admiral Wells, 9 feet below sea level in the Cambridgeshire fens near Peterborough.

**On a Bender**

Pubs are generally built on busy corners where they can attract the most business. But such plum positions are not without risk. Ask the landlord of **The Bridge Inn** at Chester, whose family were woken at 6.30am on 1st July 2012 by the arrival of not one but two cars in their lounge bar. In a freak accident on the street outside, a Vauxhall Astra and a BMW X5 collided and then ploughed on through the front wall of the pub. No one was badly hurt, although a cleaner starting her shift was greatly surprised. While one driver fled the scene, his two passengers and the second driver remained trapped in their vehicles, one on top of the other. A lack of reliable witnesses meant that nobody was successfully prosecuted. "It appears," a miffed judge remarked, "that you can drive around our city and destroy property frontages without punishment."

PUB FACT

Hinchley Wood in Surrey has one claim to fame apart from being No.49 in the book *Crap Towns*. President Gorbachev went to the pub there – after official state business was over he nipped in to The Hinchley Wood for a pub lunch on the way back to the airport. The good burghers of Hinchley Wood commemorated the fact by knocking it down 10 years later.

## Outreaches the Pub

**The White Lion** in Thakeham, West Sussex is one of a number of pubs being used for outreach work by the Church of England. Derek the vicar of the rural parish has his roots in inner-city Nottingham, and is determined that the church should break out of its self-contained religious space. So in addition to Sunday services in the house of God he turns up at the public house on the first Monday of the month "just to meet, chat, be real and have a bit of fun – with maybe a few 'god gems' thrown in." It's good to see the two central institutions of village life coming together, although there are as yet no plans to open a bar in the nave of St Mary's.

## New Superhero – Landlordman!

By the time police arrived at the scene of a public punch-up outside the Stop Inn chip shop in Stockport, it was all over. Batman and his sidekick Buzz Lightyear had broken up the brawl. By day they were Steve Lowe, landlord of **The Horse and Jockey** pub next door, and his barman Shane Lee. But on the night of 26th January 2013 they were entering into the spirit of a fancy dress party in the bar. When a fight broke out among 20 youths queuing for their fish suppers, chippy owner Aria Nouri reached for the red phone, and Batman and Buzz came running. The drunken hoodlums were so astonished at the arrival of the superhero and the spaceman that the fight quickly broke up. Greater Manchester Police recorded the incident thus: "Large scale disturbance … Batman sorted it."

## Norwich City Fans Suspected

Among the more unusual items stolen from a pub must be the 25 hand-reared canaries taken from an aviary in the garden of **The Plough and Sail** pub in Paglesham. Organised crime in the quiet Essex community is rare, and the theft in the early hours of 8th July 2012 ruffled the feathers of regulars at the Plough. The robbers came prepared, using bolt cutters to slice open the wire netting of the cage. An inside job by the birds themselves is not suspected.

## Klingon? No. Send Back

The landlord of **The Coach House** pub in Keal Cotes, Lincolnshire may have uttered a few choice Klingon curses on 16th March 2013 when he discovered that the pub had suffered a break-in. Thieves had beamed down overnight and made off with three Star Trek costumes. For the record, the following items had boldly gone: a dark red Captain Kirk outfit, another for Admiral Kirk, and one very special shark's skin uniform made for the landlord by his mother. However, after carefully studying the stolen items, the mysterious alien abductors returned them almost undamaged just three stardates later, in a binliner left by the entrance porch.

## Snakes Alive!

When Jean Yves van de Kieft, the manager of **The Montague Bar** in Edinburgh, found a rubber snake waiting for him in the cellar of the pub in March 2012, he told the barman that he wasn't paying him to play practical jokes. But the barman denied it. They returned to the cellar together to find a corn snake – a rat-catching orange and red member of the constrictor family – sitting up and taking an unwelcome interest in them. Van de Kieft managed to trap the reptile in an empty crisp box and handed it over to the Scottish SPCA. Regulars were asked not to keep asking for pints of snakebite afterwards.

PUB FACT

According to a Direct Line survey in 2009, 20% of all women will have a handbag stolen at some point in their lives, and 26% of those thefts will take place in a pub or club. Amongst 18 to 34 year olds that figure rises to 51%.

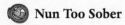 **Nun Too Sober**

Irish landlord Christy Walsh was fined 700 euros for leading 21 nuns astray. They were caught by the Garda still drinking in his pub in Listowel, Co Kerry, at 4.15am on an all-night drinking session. The nuns were in town for Nunday, a fund-raising event, an attempt on the world record for the Largest Gathering of People Dressed as Nuns, for which there is a very strict dress code – you must wear a habit, a veil, black shoes and black socks or tights. A total of 1,436 of them passed close inspection by the Guinness officials, enough for a new record.

**No Punch-Ups in the Car Park**

Saturday the 20th April 2013 saw a rare event in the recent history of licensed premises – the re-opening of a closed pub. **The Berney Arms** on the Norfolk Broads called time five months earlier, and no wonder. Drink-driving was never an issue for its customers, because driving is never an option – there are no roads to the pub, only footpaths and the navigable Breydon Water. It does have its own railway station, Berney Arms Halt,

on the Great Yarmouth to Reedham line – but it's a mile's walk from the pub itself, and only two trains in each direction stop there every day, and only on request, and only during daylight hours because there is no lighting on the single platform. The pub sits at the heart of a wildlife sanctuary.

Robbie Williams' parents, Janet and Peter, ran the The Red Lion in Stoke-on-Trent. After the Red Lion, his father went on to be the licensee at Port Vale F.C. Social Club.

### 🍾 Hart to Hart (and Back)

Many pubs are gaining trade by obtaining licences to hold wedding ceremonies. Chris and Francesca Neale, and eighty of their closest friends and family, arrived for their wedding at **The White Hart** in Great Yeldham, Essex on the appointed day of May 2011, only to find that the county council had mistakenly completed the paperwork in favour of **The White Hart** in Bocking End, 10 miles away. Rules is rules; the marriage licence said Bocking End, so the registrar and a reduced version of the wedding party drove quickly to the Bocking End pub, where a surprised landlord did his best to accommodate a makeshift ceremony. The flowers remained in Great Yeldham, so the bridesmaid carried a bunch of keys. Afterwards, the newlyweds took off their rings and raced back to Great Yeldham and their guests to do the whole thing again, complete with bouquets.

# Pub History

As we've seen in the pub names chapter, the naming of inns and taverns can be traced back hundreds of years, to the low numbers in the King Henrys and Edwards. Over the centuries, many a dark and murky conspiracy has been hatched within the walls of a tavern. They have been the scenes of heart-wrenching disaster and glorious triumph alike, but particularly the post-glorious triumph booze-up ... not to mention the post-disaster wake.

## 🍾 Grand Designs, Circa 1745

In 1745, faced with the problem of disposing of waste material from his copper smelting works, William Reeve of Bristol had the slag cast into giant black building blocks. Incorporating stonework from the city's demolished medieval gates, he built a gothic stable and laundry building for his estate, which today serves beer to builders, stone masons and other thirsty workers as **The Black Castle** pub.

The Mayflower pub in Rotherhithe has a special licence to sell both British and American postage stamps. It occupies the site of The Shippe Inn on the quay from which the pilgrim fathers sailed to America in 1620, in a building which at one time was the post office for the river community.

## Pub Revolutionary

The revolutionary principles which drove the American and French revolutions were formulated in English pubs. Several inns claim a connection with radical thinker Thomas Paine, whose 1776 pamphlet 'Common Sense' inspired the American colonies to rise up, and whose seminal 1791 book *The Rights of Man* was a defence of the violent events in France. It was a remark in 1774 by Henry Verrall, the landlord of **The White Hart** in Lewes, about Britain's involvement in the recent Seven Years War, which got Paine questioning the right of kings to govern. He was promptly sacked from his job as a customs officer for sedition, and emigrated to America in the company of Benjamin Franklin in 1774. But the beer in the colonies wasn't good (no change in over 200 years then). He returned to England in 1787, and began work on *The Rights of Man* over a drink or two in the pubs of Islington, notably **The Red Lion** and **The Angel**.

##  Make it a Double

Francis Crick and his research colleague James Watson worked in Cambridge University's Cavendish Laboratories and regularly took their lunch breaks in **The Eagle** pub nearby. At lunchtime on 28th February 1953 Crick arrived late, and declared, as he went over to the bench in the back bar where Watson and other colleagues had started without him, "Gentlemen, we have discovered the secret of life." Crick and Watson had identified the double-helix model of DNA structure, the single most important scientific discovery of the 20th century. The bench is still there, available to great thinkers and drinkers in the Eagle today.

## The Eagle's Greatest Hit

The site of **The Eagle** in Hoxton has a long history. It opened as a teetotal tea garden but became a music hall in 1825. A young Marie Lloyd performed there in the 1880s. By then the Eagle was a rough joint in a rough neighbourhood where rough locals would pawn anything for a rough drink. The Eagle was immortalised in a popular song of 1855:

> Up and down the City Road
> In and out The Eagle
> That's the way the money goes
> Pop goes the weasel

Popping meant pawning, and a weasel was a tailor's iron. Such dissipated living offended late Victorian morals, and in 1882 the Salvation Army bought the music hall and turned it into a centre for Christian worship. This so outraged the locals that they drowned out the Army's hymns with their own bawdy songs – including, perhaps, 'Pop Goes the Weasel'. The short-lived centre closed in 1901 when it was demolished and the present pub of the same name built in its place.

## Brahms and Listing to Starboard

The RMS *Mauretania* had a long and distinguished career as a transatlantic liner, until its demise in the breaker's yard at Rosyth in 1935. Its luxurious fixtures and fittings were then auctioned off, and many of them found new leases of life as opulent pub interiors. **The Oak Bar** in Dublin has oak timber panels from the ship and in Bristol, fittingly, **The Mauretania Bar** bought extensively from its namesake. The mahogany panelling of the lounge bar was the first-class passengers' library. Although the pub changed its name recently to **Java Bristol**, it retains the Mauretania's proud bow lettering above its entrance.

## The King in the Car Park

On 25th August 1651, one of the last battles of the English Civil War was fought – at a pub. Landlord and customers of **The Boar's Head** on Wigan Road, Standish (built in 1450) had an extremely close view as the Battle of Wigan Lane raged around them. The result was a convincing rout of Charles II and his Scottish mercenaries at the hands of the Roundheads. After two further defeats (at Uxton and Worcester), the king fled to France, and Britain became a republic with Cromwell at the helm until Charles's restoration in 1660. The Boar's Head survived all these dramatic events.

## That's Four Guineas and a Grote, Guv

A lot of pubs try to keep up with the times. A change of name, a change of décor – it all helps to keep the place fresh and in the news. Not so **The King's Head** in Islington. The landlord Dan Crawford was implacable in his opposition to the introduction of decimal currency, and for 40 years after the 1971 decimalisation, he insisted on selling drinks in (the equivalent of) old money with an antique cash till. (For the record, two pints in 2008 would set you back six pounds and 18 shillings.) Only the introduction of computerised tills put an end to the practice, which outlived Dan himself by several years.

## Hopping Mad in Hopping Kent

On 3rd September 1947, **The Kent Arms** in the hop-growing town of Paddock Wood in Kent, changed its name to **The John Brunt V.C.** It remains the only pub named after a recipient of the Victoria Cross. John Brunt, who was also awarded the Military Cross, was killed by a stray mortar shell in Italy on 10th December 1944, only a day after the heroic acts which won him his V.C. He was 22. In 1997, 50 years after the last renaming of the pub, new owners changed the name to **The Hopping Hooden Horse**, their insensitivity to local pride resulting in a widespread boycott of the Brunt, as it remained known by locals. When the pub changed hands again in 2001, it became the John Brunt V.C. once more.

## The Footman Cometh...

As London's streets broadened, the need for the traditional footman diminished. Their job had been to go on foot ahead of their employer's vehicle and clear the way through the crowded lanes, cutting a swathe through the stinking proletariat. Height was an advantage for such a servant, as was a stout stick and some choice words. By the end of the century the Marquis of Queensbury was one of the last aristocrats to keep such a member of staff, not so much a practical requirement as a status symbol. One of his favourites was able to maintain a steady eight miles an hour as he ran ahead of the Marquis' carriage. And when the footman retired and bought a pub – **The Running Horse** – to keep him in his old age, he proudly renamed it (**I Am**) **The Only Running Footman**. It is the longest pub name in London, and one of the oddest.

## Raising Hull

It's not surprising that so many pubs should claim associations with an event so nationwide and so divisive as the English Civil War. One ancient pub, **Ye Olde White Hart** in Hull, can claim to be where the whole thing started. On 23rd April 1642, in an upstairs room still known as the Plotters' Parlour, a group of parliamentarians agreed to close the city gates against the approaching king of England. The ensuing unsuccessful siege of Hull by the king was the first confrontation of a bruising conflict which continued off and on for 17 years. If you visit the Hart you can see not only the parlour but – in a glass case in another room – a human skull of uncertain date discovered in the attic after a fire in 1881.

**Train and Coaching Inn**

The advent of the railways caused an irreversible decline in coach business and the pubs that serviced it. The Stockton and Darlington Railway opened on 27th September 1825, and the short branch to Yarm three weeks later on 17th October. After a brief opening ceremony everyone adjourned to the pub – **The New Inn**, an early and direct example of the new threat to coaching inns – the railway pub. Built beside the Yarm tracks, the New Inn opened for business the same day as the railway and soon changed its name to **The Station Inn**, a sign of things to come. It still stands, now called **The Cleveland Bay**.

 **Up**

Two of Manchester's oldest buildings are pubs. The half-timbered **Old Wellington Inn** occupies premises originally built as a draper's shop in 1552. At ninety degrees to it in Shambles Square sits **Sinclair's Oyster Bar**, originally erected in the 18th century as **John Shaw's Punch House**. Both buildings are rare survivors of Manchester's past after the blitz of World War II and began life in a row as one side of the old Shambles, a narrow lane. In 1974, the whole lane on which the pubs sat was underpinned with concrete and raised to accommodate the Arndale Centre. Then, in the wake of the IRA bomb which destroyed the centre of Manchester on 15th June 1996, Sinclair's and the Wellington were dismantled brick by brick and beam by beam, and reassembled in their new right-angle relationship some 300 metres to the north of their original position.

"Give my people plenty of beer, good beer, and cheap beer, and you will have no revolution among them."

*Queen Victoria*

## 🍾 Light Ales, CAMRA, Action

Kruger Cavanagh was a bodyguard of Irish president De Valera who bought a pub on the Dingle peninsula as a retirement plan. Over a pint or two in **Kruger's Bar** at Dunquin on 16th March 1971, four beer-loving friends on holiday in the area decided to fight back against the rise of keg beer. That night, CAMRA, the Campaign for the Revitalisation of Real Ale was born. CAMRA's first AGM was held in **The Rose Inn** at Nuneaton a year later. At a time when traditional pubs are closing down altogether, we owe a huge debt to CAMRA, now the Campaign for Real Ale for reminding us what a proper pub should be.

## 🎸 Public Pubs

The year 1973 marked the end of a strange period in British licensing laws which stretched back to the World War I. As vast armaments factories sprang up around the country, the government nationalised pubs and breweries in three critical parts of the country where a reliable (and sober) workforce was essential to the war effort – Enfield, the Cromarty Firth and Carlisle. In Carlisle the state took over four breweries and 235 pubs. Many beloved old drinking dens were demolished, replaced by a new style of state-owned public house which became the model for pub buildings for much of the 20th century. Opening hours were restricted and for the first few years there was a 'no treating' policy – it was illegal to buy a round for your colleagues. On the plus side, beer prices were regulated and relatively cheap in state pubs. In 1971, Edward Heath ended the scheme, selling the premises off to the big brewery chains. The last to go were in Cumbria, where the one remaining Carlisle State Brewery went to Theakston's in 1973.

###  Pub Fight…Involving Machine Guns

The Battle of Graveney Marsh, the last military action on British soil against an invading force, was fought by soldiers in a pub. One might question the wisdom of billeting men from the 1st London Irish Rifles in **The Sportsman Inn** on the Graveney marshes. But there they were on the night of 27th September 1940 when they heard the unmistakable sound of a Junkers Ju 88 bomber crash-landing nearby. They rushed out to take prisoners, only to find that for the German aircrew the war was far from over. They had armed themselves with the plane's machine guns and were resisting the capture of themselves and what turned out to be a top secret new version of their aircraft. After a brief firefight the Luftwaffe men were all taken alive. The valuable prize was sent to Farnborough airfield, and the fighting London Irish returned to their pub.

### Kings in the Queen's

**The Queen's Head** in Newton, Cambridge, is used to hosting nobility. In the 1960s the Shah of Persia came in for a pub lunch. And before that at the dawn of the 20th century, two cousins popped in for a drink and chat. If the conversation had gone differently then, the course of world history might have changed; they were King George V of Britain and Kaiser Wilhelm of Germany.

### Do Drop In

**The Snowdrop Inn**, nestling below chalk cliffs in Lewes on the Sussex coast, celebrates not the first flower of spring but the worst winter disaster in British history. On Christmas Eve 1836 snow began to fall heavily, and continued for several days. The offshore winds swept up the steep cliffs, carving a large overhanging cornice of snow and ice. On the 27th of December it could no longer support its own weight and crashed down onto a row of houses below. Eight lives were lost, and seven houses were destroyed completely. The Snowdrop Inn was built soon afterwards on the site.

> I have heard him assert, that a tavern chair was the throne of human felicity. "As soon," said he, "as I enter the door of a tavern, I experience an oblivion of care, and a freedom from solicitude: when I am seated, I find the master courteous, and the servants obsequious to my call; anxious to know and ready to supply my wants : wine there exhilarates my spirits, and prompts me to free conversation and an interchange of discourse with those whom I most love."
>
> *Samuel Johnson*

## Aussie PM Downs a Yard

**The Turf Tavern** in Oxford sits just outside the old city walls – the right side to be if, like its 19th-century gambling patrons, you were likely to be breaking the law. And yet there's something about the pub that attracts the world's leading lawmakers. In 1963, as a student, future Australian prime minister Bob Hawke set a world record here by downing a yard of ale (about two and a half pints) in 11 seconds. It would be nice to think that such a talent came in handy during his years in office. One skill was emphatically NOT demonstrated by future US president Bill Clinton, who was a student here in the late 1960s. The Turf is the pub in which Clinton "did not inhale" marijuana. Did not.

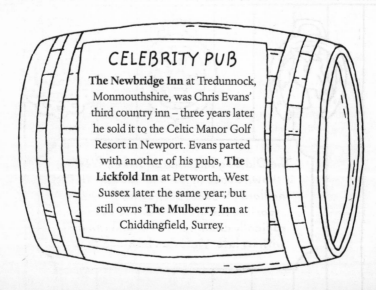

### CELEBRITY PUB

**The Newbridge Inn** at Tredunnock, Monmouthshire, was Chris Evans' third country inn – three years later he sold it to the Celtic Manor Golf Resort in Newport. Evans parted with another of his pubs, **The Lickfold Inn** at Petworth, West Sussex later the same year; but still owns **The Mulberry Inn** at Chiddingfield, Surrey.

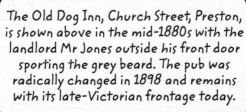

The Old Dog Inn, Church Street, Preston, is shown above in the mid-1880s with the landlord Mr Jones outside his front door sporting the grey beard. The pub was radically changed in 1898 and remains with its late-Victorian frontage today.